THE WORLD *needs* MORE OF IT

What is that one thing you need the most in life??

ABHISHEK BHATT

BlueRose ONE.com
Stories Matter
NewDelhi • London

BLUEROSE PUBLISHERS
India | U.K.

BlueRose ONE.com
Stories Matter
NewDelhi • London

For permissions requests or inquiries regarding this publication, please contact:

BLUEROSE PUBLISHERS
www.BlueRoseONE.com
info@bluerosepublishers.com
+91 8882 898 898
+4407342408967

ISBN: 978-93-6261-418-6

Cover design: Abhishek Bhatt
Typesetting: Namrata Saini

First Edition: December 2024

Contents

Preface .... *v*

Thank you .... *vii*

Introduction .... *xi*

Chapter 1: Life is an Art 1

Chapter 2: Be Your Own Friend 13

Chapter 3: We Always Have a Choice 24

Chapter 4: Satisfaction over Success 36

Chapter 5: Be a Fighter 54

Chapter 6: God is Not Listening to Me 68

Chapter 7: Life is a Beautiful Gift 76

Chapter 8: Patience is the key 96

Chapter 9: Are You a Good Listener? 110

Chapter 10: Beyond First Impression 123

Chapter 11: One More Life 129

Preface

Fear, anxiety, and stress are natural responses to the uncertainties and obstacles that come our way.

Acknowledging these emotions is important because it validates our humanity and reminds us that we are alive, with a capacity to feel and react.

However, what truly matters is how we navigate and transcend these feelings.

Instead of letting them to paralyze us or hinder our progress, we should strive to find ways to overcome them. It's crucial to recognize that these feelings, in moderation, can be a driving force for personal growth and achievement. They can push us out of our comfort zones, encouraging us to take risks, pursue our aspirations and discover our true potential.

Ultimately, the key lies in embracing these emotions as a part of our human experience while consciously striving to maintain a positive mindset and a proactive approach. It is about harnessing our inner strength and resilience to face adversity, learn from it, and emerge stronger and wiser.

By doing so, we can transform our perspective and embrace life with a renewed sense of purpose and possibility. It is through this process that we can truly live a fulfilling and meaningful life.

May this book serve as a channel for spreading love, hope, and self-empowerment. May it be a testament to the power of faith and the transformative potential of embracing positivity in every aspect of life.

Thank you

To the almighty God, who has given me the ability to see positive in every situation. Throughout the process of writing this book, I have felt the presence of a higher power guiding me, providing me with the wisdom, clarity, and creativity to express my thoughts and ideas effectively.

My ultimate goal with this book is to make a difference in the lives of those who read it. Whether it is a single person or many, I will feel truly blessed if my thoughts and insights can bring about a positive transformation in someone's life. Even if this book provides solace, encouragement, or a glimmer of hope to just one individual, it will have fulfilled its purpose.

I am humbled and grateful to dedicate this book to every person I have had the privilege of crossing paths with on my journey. Each encounter, whether fleeting or enduring, has left an indelible mark on my life.

I am honored to dedicate this book to my beloved wife, who has been an unwavering presence by my side through every twist and turn of this literary journey. Her unconditional support and boundless love have been the guiding light that has propelled me forward, instilling in me the confidence and determination to overcome any obstacle that came my way.

Throughout the process of writing this book, my wife has been my rock and my most trusted confidante. From the inception of the rough drafts to the final touches, she has been there as my first editor, offering her insightful feedback and invaluable suggestions. With each chapter I completed, she was the one eagerly awaiting to delve into the pages. Her belief in my writing and her willingness to accompany me on this creative journey have been a constant source of motivation, driving me to push beyond my limits and refine my work. Her keen eye for detail and her ability to bring out the best in my ideas have shaped this book into what it has become.

To my Mother & Father, who have stood by my side through the highs and lows, your love and support have been a constant source of strength. Your belief in me, even when I doubted myself has been an inspiration on this journey, reminding me the importance of unity, strength, and unconditional love.

To my friends, who have shared countless moments of laughter and tears, you have been my pillars of support and my chosen family. Through thick and thin, we have celebrated triumphs together and found solace in one another's embrace during times of sorrow. This is an expression of gratitude for the bond we have nurtured, for the countless memories we have created, and for the understanding and empathy that have defined our friendship.

To all the failures I have faced along the way. Those moments of disappointment, setbacks, and shattered dreams have been invaluable teachers. It is through these failures that I have discovered the true essence of growth and the importance of learning from life's challenges. To remind me that failure is not an endpoint, but a stepping stone towards growth and eventual success. At the same time, I dedicate this book to the success I have achieved. It has served as both milestones and reminders of the ephemeral nature of triumph, and taught me the importance of humility and gratitude. Success is not a solitary achievement but a collective effort, and a reminder to remain grounded and humble in the face of achievements.

Furthermore, I dedicate this book to the deceptions and betrayals I have experienced. While painful these encounters have taught me invaluable lessons about trust, discernment, and the importance of surrounding oneself with genuine connections. They have fueled my determination to rise above deceit and to cultivate relationships built on integrity and authenticity.

This book is dedicated to all those who have influenced my life, both positively and negatively.

Introduction

As we all know, life is a tapestry woven with countless encounters, discussions, and varied viewpoints. Each person carries their own beliefs and perceptions about life's circumstances and challenges. Like everyone else, I have my own set of views, a unique perspective on certain aspects of life that I wish to share. My hope is that these insights can bring about a positive difference in your life, as well as the lives of others.

Within every individual, I believe there lies an optimistic soul-a beacon of positivity that seeks to find the silver lining in every situation, no matter how dire. I firmly believe that no one can definitively determine what is truly the "best" or the "worst" in life. This view comes from understanding that as humans, we experience a wide range of emotions: love, betrayal, happiness, sorrow, joy, success, failure, and countless others.

Sometimes we find ourselves uplifted by the simple sight of an elderly person playing with a small puppy at the corner of the street. Other times, we may be overcome with sadness due to seemingly insignificant reasons. However, it is important to recognize that what we perceive as negative or undesirable may, in fact, hold the hidden blessings and lessons for our personal growth. I firmly believe that every experience we encounter serves a purpose, even if it may not align with our immediate desires and expectations.

Guided by this perspective, I strive to live life with an open mind, embracing the power of positivity. I approach each situation with a willingness to learn and understand, even when faced with challenges and setbacks. By doing so, I endeavor to uncover the inherent beauty and potential within every situation.

Of course, this optimistic approach does not diminish the very real struggles we face. Life throws us plenty of curveballs, and acknowledging them is essential for personal growth and resilience. However, my belief is that by embracing positivity, we can navigate through life's trials with greater strength and clarity.

Adopting a positive perspective enables us to find solace in the darkest moments, to seek solutions instead of dwelling on problems, and to offer support and empathy to those around us. It empowers us to cultivate gratitude for the blessings we often overlook and to recognize the potential for growth and self-improvement in every experience.

In a world that can often seem inundated with negativity, embracing a positive outlook is a beacon of hope.

It invites us to see the good in ourselves, in others, and in the world at large. By sharing these thoughts, I hope to inspire others to adopt a similar perspective—one that acknowledges the challenges of life but chooses to focus on the light that shines within each of us.

Together, let us foster a community that thrives on positivity, understanding, and compassion. Let us uncover the hidden optimism within ourselves and encourage others to do the same. By doing so, we can create a ripple effect of positive change, transforming our lives and the lives of those we encounter along the way.

Chapter 1

Life is an Art

In our journey through life, we encounter various difficulties and challenges. They are an integral part of our existence, and how we navigate and overcome them truly reflects the art of living. Just like an artist embarking on the creation of a beautiful masterpiece, we must exercise great care and deliberation in choosing the right canvas, brushes, and colors. Each element plays a vital role in shaping the final outcome.

The process begins with choosing the appropriate canvas, symbolizing the foundation upon which our dreams and aspirations will be realized. This canvas represents the environment, circumstances, and opportunities that shape our path. By selecting wisely, we set the stage for our endeavors.

Next, we consider the brushes, which represent the tools and skills we employ to navigate challenges.

We must be mindful of choosing the right brushes that enable us to make precise strokes and bring our vision to life. These brushes encompass our knowledge, abilities, and strategies that help us overcome obstacles and make progress.

Moreover, the mix of colors we select signifies the attitudes, perspectives, and emotions that we infuse into our journey. Just as a painter chooses colors to evoke specific feelings and convey meaning, we must be intentional in cultivating positive mindsets and embracing resilience. The rough texture of canvas representing the challenges, urges us to apply bold strokes of color that transform our lives. It is through this thoughtful selection of rich shades that we can bring vibrancy and depth to our lives.

However, the true essence of creating something remarkable lies not only in the technical aspects but also in the originality and authenticity of our creation.

In the world of art, it is not uncommon to find individuals who replicate the works of others. They meticulously reproduce the strokes and details, achieving a perfect imitation. Yet, despite their skill, their creation remains nothing more than a copy, lacking the essence of originality. However, there are those who opt to tap into their own wellspring of imagination, using it as a guiding force to create something truly unique—a genuine masterpiece.

The same principle applies to our lives. We can choose to follow in the footsteps of others, merely imitating their actions and decisions. While we may achieve a certain level of success by replicating their paths, our achievements will always be shadowed by the absence of authenticity. Alternatively, we can harness the power of our own creativity, trusting in our unique perspective to forge a path that is entirely our own. By doing so, we have the opportunity to craft an original life, one that reflects our true essence and individuality.

It is not uncommon to hear people express their inability to draw. What's more disheartening is the fact that many individuals do not possess the desire to learn this artistic skill. Strangely enough, this same phenomenon extends beyond the realm of art and applies to our everyday lives. Just as some are hesitant from painting their visions on canvas, many of us cagey to pursue our dreams, fearing the possibility of failure.

If we pause to reflect, we will realize that none of us has ever envisioned a bleak future for ourselves. Instead, we all harbor dreams of a life filled with joy, success, and fulfillment. However, to bring those dreams to fruition, my friend, we must take on the role of painters and wield our brushes accordingly.

Just as an artist selects the colors that resonate with their imagination, we too must carefully choose the hues that align with our dreams and aspirations. These colors represent our goals, values, and deepest desires. It is through these shades that we will paint the canvas of our lives.

To create the life we envision, it is essential to recognize that each brushstroke matters. Our actions, decisions, and choices are akin to the strokes of a brush on a canvas. Each one contributes to the larger picture, shaping our experiences and determining the outcome.

In order to paint a life that reflects our dreams, we must be willing to learn and grow. Just as aspiring artists invest time and effort in honing their skills, we too must dedicate ourselves to personal development. This entails acquiring new knowledge, embracing challenges, and expanding our horizons.

While it may be tempting to sit back and hope for a masterpiece to materialize magically, it is in our hands to create the life we desire. We have the power to pick up the brush and apply it with purpose, intention, and resilience. It is through our actions, guided by the vibrant colors of our dreams, that we can transform our aspirations into a beautiful reality.

Life is a canvas filled with an array of emotions, much like the vibrant colors in a painting. Just as each color holds its own significance, every emotion we experience plays a pivotal role in shaping our journey and building our future.

Similar to the diverse palette of colors, emotions come in various shades and intensities. One such example is the color red, which evokes strong emotions and holds contrasting symbolism. It can represent danger and violence, yet it also signifies love and passion. Bold and intense, the color red commands attention and leaves a lasting impression.

Another color with its own distinct characteristics is green. Often associated with coolness, green symbolizes growth and new beginnings. It is closely connected to nature and the earth, representing harmony and vitality. However, green can also be linked to jealousy and envy, showcasing the dual nature of emotions and their multifaceted impact.

In the realm of emotions, there are also neutral colors, such as black. Black is often associated with power, elegance, and sophistication. It exudes a sense of mystery and intrigue. However, it can also be linked to negativity and darkness, carrying connotations of evil or the unknown.

Contrasting with the depth of black, white emerges as a color representing purity, peace, and goodness. It embodies a sense of serenity and simplicity. However, even white has its shades of complexity, as it can also be associated with sadness or mourning, reminding us of life's inevitable losses and transitions.

Just as an artist carefully selects and blends colors to relate a visually captivating masterpiece, we too have the power to navigate and express our emotions. Understanding the significance and nuances of different emotions enables us to make conscious choices and respond appropriately to life's circumstances.

Just as every color possesses both positive and negative attributes, each emotional experience holds its own spectrum of effects. Some emotions, such as love, hatred, and anger, exhibit great intensity and can significantly impact our lives. These powerful emotions have the potential to drive us towards deep connections, ignite a fiery passion, or fuel conflicts and animosity.

On the other hand, there are emotions of a more moderate nature, such as pleasure, satisfaction, and amusement. These emotions bring about a sense of contentment, joy, and lightheartedness. They may not possess the same level of intensity as their stronger counterparts, but they still contribute to the rich tapestry of human experiences.

It is important to recognize that emotions are multidimensional in nature. Their magnitude or intensity may vary from person to person and from situation to situation. What may elicit a strong emotional response in one individual may have a milder impact on another. Additionally, emotions can evolve and transform over time as we navigate through life's experiences and grow as individuals.

While emotions have the potential to influence our lives, we possess the remarkable ability to navigate and manage their effects. Through self-awareness, emotional intelligence, and conscious choice, we can maintain a healthy equilibrium amidst the ebb and flow of emotions. By recognizing the positive and negative aspects of each emotion, we can harness their energy in constructive ways and mitigate their potential harm.

Peace and calmness, often regarded as neutral emotions, possess a unique power to influence the intensity of other emotions. In the realm of colors, white serves as a key component in creating lighter shades. The whiter is added, the lighter the shade becomes. Despite its appearance as a seemingly weak color, white has the ability to transform the intensity of any other color, while no color can lighten or darken it, not even black. This quality attributes a sense of purity to white, making it analogous to the emotions of peace and calmness.

In our daily lives, we can observe this phenomenon in action. When confronted with intense anger, incorporating a touch of calmness can noticeably diminish its intensity. This principle applies to other emotions as well. By introducing a measure of peace and tranquility into our emotional state, we can alleviate the heightened intensity of various emotions.

Just as an artist skillfully balances colors on a canvas, we too can harmonize our emotions by consciously blending peace and calmness into the mix. This practice allows us to navigate the complexities of our emotional landscape with greater ease. By embracing the pure essence of peace and calmness, we can cultivate emotional equilibrium and foster a more tranquil and fulfilling existence.

Embarking on the creation of a masterpiece in life necessitates a deep understanding of the intricacies of emotions. Much like the process of crafting a drawing, initial stages may seem uncertain and perplexing, as if the path ahead remains obscured. However, as we commence the journey of refining our creation, adding symmetry and infusing vibrant colors, the image begins to emerge, mirroring the beauty we envisioned.

The artistry of crafting a picture unfolds in a deliberate step-by-step manner. It commences with sketching the rough outlines, allowing room for exploration and adjustment. If errors arise, we courageously erase them and begin anew, persisting until satisfaction is achieved. With the foundation in place, contemplation ensues regarding which sections to fill and with what hues. Deliberation may be required to determine the appropriate intensity of each color, sometimes even necessitating the exploration of various shades within the same color palette.

However, the true magic lies in achieving a harmonious balance among the colors. Skillfully blending them together becomes paramount, as layers of one color atop another may disrupt the visual harmony we seek. Through seamless blending, colors merge effortlessly, imparting a sense of cohesion and visual perfection to the artwork.

Similar to the artistry of painting, the journey of creating a masterpiece in life involves careful consideration of emotions. We learn to navigate their variations, selecting the most suitable shades to color our experiences. Each emotion holds a place of significance, and like colors on a canvas, they must find equilibrium and synergy with one another. By artfully blending our emotions, we forge a path towards inner harmony and a life adorned with the beauty of emotional balance.

The parallel between painting and real life continues, albeit with a subtle distinction. Unlike in painting, where we have the ability to erase and start anew, in real life, we cannot simply undo our actions or choices. However, what we do possess is the power to shift the direction of our imagination and create something even more remarkable.

Each step we take in life is irrevocable, yet the beauty lies in our capacity to learn, adapt, and grow from our experiences. When a stroke on the canvas of life doesn't meet our expectations, we have the opportunity to recalibrate our mindset, adjust our course, and channel our imagination into new and inspiring directions. By doing so, we can transform our initial creation into something even more magnificent.

The adage, "*You cannot undo a move, but you can make the next one better,*" encapsulates this sentiment perfectly. It reminds us that while we cannot alter the past, we have the power to shape our future. Each decision we make, each action we take, presents an opportunity to refine our path, learn from our mistakes, and make choices that align more closely with our vision and aspirations.

Embracing this perspective allows us to approach life as an ongoing masterpiece, ever-evolving and filled with potential. Rather than dwelling on the past or fixating on what cannot be changed, we can focus our energy and creativity on making each subsequent move better than the last.

This mindset empowers us to cultivate resilience, adaptability, and a willingness to explore new possibilities.

Life is an expansive canvas, a tapestry of vivid hues, profound emotions, and boundless possibilities. From the moment we enter this world, we are endowed with the innate ability to paint our own extraordinary existence. Our journey commences with a blank canvas, awaiting our personal touch. In this grand design, we are blessed with the divine gift of a vibrant palette, encapsulated within our brilliant minds and passionate hearts. Our bodies, akin to finely crafted brushes, serve as the tools with which we navigate this artistic voyage.

The choices we make, the strokes we take, determine the essence of our creation. Will we replicate the strokes of others, mirroring their experiences and paths? Or shall we summon the depths of our imagination, daring to breathe life into an authentic masterpiece that is uniquely ours? The decision lies within us, beckoning us to forge our own narrative upon the canvas of life.

Amidst this artistic odyssey, I offer a secret weapon— embrace the power of white. Symbolizing purity and clarity, white possesses an inherent ability to illuminate and enhance every stroke upon our canvas. It fosters harmony, infusing our creation with balance and light. By weaving the luminous strands of white into our tapestry, we create a tapestry that captivates and resonates.

So, my fellow artists of life, let your imagination unfurl its wings and unleash a symphony of colors upon your canvas. Embrace the uncharted realms of your dreams and aspirations, for it is within this realm that your true masterpiece awaits. Paint boldly, embracing the unique brushstrokes that emanate from your soul. Let your creation be a testament to the boundless spirit that resides within you. Embrace the vastness of life's canvas and breathe life into your extraordinary masterpiece.

Chapter 2

Be Your Own Friend

There comes a time in everyone's life when we experience a sense of demotivation, which can be a challenging and disheartening phase. During these challenging periods, it can be incredibly difficult to think positively, which often leads to a cascade of negative emotions such as depression, anxiety, frustration, and hopelessness. It is at such moments that we actively seek motivation to uplift our spirits and regain a sense of purpose and drive.

Let's take the example of COVID-19. A few years ago, a pandemic swept across the globe, fundamentally altering the way we live. The impact was profound, and among the most immediate effects was a staggering loss of jobs. As businesses shuttered and economies ground to a halt, millions found themselves without a source of income. Fear and demotivation were natural reactions to such an abrupt and severe disruption.

During this time of widespread job loss and economic uncertainty, many individuals felt the crushing weight of the crisis. Some were overwhelmed by the burden and struggled to cope with the new reality. The sudden stop to their means of earning left them feeling hopeless and unsure of the future.

However, in the midst of this turmoil, there were also those who saw opportunity where others saw only despair. These individuals used the pandemic as a catalyst for reinvention. They adapted to the changing landscape, finding new ways to generate income and sustain themselves. Whether by pivoting to new industries, learning new skills, or starting their own ventures, these resilient people turned a disaster into a chance for growth and transformation.

To find motivation, many individuals turn to external sources such as reading motivational quotes, watching inspiring movies, listening to motivational speakers, or seeking guidance from counselors. Following these sources can be a positive and constructive step. They have the power to inspire and encourage us to take action, overcome obstacles, and pursue our goals by offering insights, stories and new perspectives that may resonate with us and help us regain a sense of purpose and direction in life.

However, it is important to recognize that the most significant, enduring, and long-lasting motivation comes from within ourselves. No other person can truly understand our unique circumstances, aspirations, capabilities, experiences, and desires as intimately as we do. We possess the inherent power to motivate ourselves even during the most difficult times.

Discovering self-motivation may seem dismaying, but it is an achievable process which requires self-realization and introspection. It is a process of acknowledging our strengths and propagating a positive mindset. It is an exercise where we have to take time to understand our values, passions, and goals. What are the factors that truly excite us? What are the core reasons behind our ambitions? By exploring these factors, one can tap into his or her innate motivation.

I believe this self-motivation is not a difficult task to accomplish; it just requires one key element and that is "Talking to oneself and reminding oneself of their childhood dreams."

Childhood is a stage where we are full of dreams and aspirations. It is a time when we envision our future, imagine what we want to become and plan our lives accordingly. Whether it's aspiring to be a doctor, an artist, or pursuing a particular field of study, we start building a roadmap towards those dreams through our studies, courses, artistic endeavors, and more. Some individuals are able to achieve their dreams, while others get detoured in the race of life.

There are several factors that affect our achievements and goals. As we navigate through the journey of life, we often get caught up in the daily responsibilities and obligations that come our way. The pressure of competition, insecurity, and social expectations can take the center stage, causing us to lose sight of our initial plans and dreams.

Now the question comes, what can we do to rekindle our motivation?

According to my experience, to reignite our motivation, it is essential to reconnect with our childhood dreams.

How can we do it?

By taking time to have an introspective conversation with ourselves, reflecting on those aspirations that once ignited our passion. Reminding ourselves of the goals we set for ourselves and the reasons behind them. Rediscovering the excitement and enthusiasm we had during those early years.

By embracing self-motivation, we can reestablish a sense of purpose, regain control over our lives, and find the drive to overcome obstacles and challenges. This introspective dialogue allows us to realign our focus, redirect our efforts, and prioritize what truly matters to us. It empowers us to break free from the societal pressure and expectations, and helps us reconnect with our genuine desires.

Remember this:

The motivation that comes from within is powerful because it is rooted in our own unique values and dreams. It fuels our drive to pursue what truly brings us joy and fulfillment.

In today's world, it is not uncommon to witness individuals attending concerts featuring motivational speakers or seeking guidance from counselors and emerging from these experiences feeling motivated, inspired, and uplifted, exclaiming phrases such as "I will do it," "I will win," or "I will not give up." Similarly, individuals experience a positive shift in their mindset after a few sessions with a counselor.

Let me ask you something:

What do they say that we start feeling motivated or inspired?

Why do we start following them?

Why do we need them to say that we can do it?

What exactly is there in the motivational seminars, classes, motivational movies or motivational quotes that make us feel motivated?

People willingly invest in tickets for motivational seminars or pay substantial fees for counseling sessions. However, in my opinion, these sources of motivation may not offer anything new that we don't already know.

The truth is that the principles of achieving success and fulfilling one's dreams are not hidden secrets. Most of us are already aware that hard work, honesty, dedication, focus, and consistency are key factors in achieving our goals. The knowledge of these fundamental principles is not limited to a select few but rather widely acknowledged by society. It is a commonly held belief that if we diligently apply ourselves to a task, remain focused, and persevere without allowing distractions from worldly affairs, we will ultimately achieve our goals and fulfil our dreams.

One of the greatest benefits we receive while attending motivational seminars is the electrifying energy and the collective desire of all individuals present to gain motivation and inspiration. The environment is filled with like-minded people who share a common goal of seeking personal growth and empowerment. This atmosphere can be incredibly uplifting.

Let's consider the example of a counseling session:

During a counseling session, the counselor typically spends a significant portion of the time listening attentively to you, about forty-five minutes out of a one-hour session. In the remaining fifteen minutes, the counselor provides guidance and suggests actions for you to take to address your problems or challenges.

While it may appear that the counselor is offering you new solutions or ideas, in reality, the basis of those suggestions often stems from the information you shared during the initial forty-five minutes of speaking. It was you who provided the counselor with insights into your situation or ideas that were already within your knowledge. Through open and honest communication, you express your thoughts, concerns, and experiences. In the process of narrating your story and describing your challenges, you often reveal potential solutions. The counselor's role is to actively listen, ask probing questions, and facilitate the exploration of these insights.

While you may already have some understanding of the solutions, the counselor's input serves a vital purpose. By listening to you and offering guidance, the counselor reaffirms your own knowledge and capabilities.

Here it is important to clarify that my intention is not to discredit the value of attending motivational seminars or seeking guidance from others. Motivating and inspiring individuals is a noble and impactful endeavor and many people dedicate themselves to this purpose. The point I want to make is that before seeking external sources of motivation or counseling, cultivate the habit to engage in self-reflection and become your own source of motivation and guidance.

You have the power to be your own motivator and counselor. Before reaching out to others, take the time to have a meaningful conversation with yourself. Acknowledge your dreams, aspirations, and goals. Remember the decisions you have made for your life and the plans you have set in motion. Rather than waiting for anyone else saying, "You can do it," take on the responsibility of being the one who declares, "I have decided it, I have planned for it, and I will do it."

"It is crucial to understand that your own voice, determination, and self-belief are the foundations upon which success is built"

Motivation and demotivation can be influenced by various factors that play a significant role in our lives. To name a few, these factors include our friends, colleagues, relationships, work culture, environment, and the discussions we have with the people around us.

Just like we choose to attend motivational seminars to experience a positive environment, we also have the power to choose the kind of environment we want to live in and the type of people we want to surround ourselves with.

It is crucial for our motivation and overall well-being to choose the right environment and the right people to surround ourselves with. The company we keep can significantly impact our mindset, attitude, and aspirations. While positive, supportive, and like-minded individuals can inspire and uplift us, providing a healthier environment for our progress. On the other hand, negative influences and toxic relationships can drain our energy and hinder our personal growth.

It is requisite to seek out individuals who encourage, challenge, and inspire us to be our best selves.

As human beings, we have an innate need to make connections, form relationships, and trust others. However, in the journey of life, we often forget the importance of trusting ourselves and taking care of our own well-being. This goes beyond physical care and delves into the realm of mental well-being. We forget to be our own friends. Being our own friend means following the practices of self-compassion, self-acceptance, and self-trust. When we become our own friends, we create a foundation of self-support and resilience that allows us to navigate the ups and downs of life more effectively.

Throughout our lives, we have been our most constant companions. Taking care of mental well-being involves the practice of taking time to engage in introspection and self-reflection, particularly when embarking on new endeavors. Whether it is starting a new course, pursuing a new job or business opportunity, or entering into a new relationship, seeking your own advice is very important. Taking the time to assess your thoughts, feelings, and doubts enables you to make informed decisions and evaluate whether a particular path aligns with your goals and values.

"It is you who can provide yourself with the best advice tailored to your specific situation."

Imagine having a daily conversation with your greatest cheerleader–yourself for at least thirty minutes. To remind you that you are doing "just fine". By regularly talking to yourself you can gain insights into your own patterns, beliefs, and strengths that will lead to a better understanding of yourself. However, some individuals may prefer shorter or longer sessions, that is why it is important to find a routine that works best for you and aligns with your personal needs and circumstances.

Furthermore, consider self-talk as a form of self-care and stress relief. It helps in releasing pent-up emotions, reducing anxiety, and managing stress. Similar to medication, the practice of regular self-talk can promote mindfulness and a greater sense of inner peace.

To maintain a daily dose of motivation, we have to practice it consistently and religiously.

Motivation is like a voice from within or from someone else that encourages us with the belief that "we can do it". It is my humble recommendation that, if you genuinely want to be someone's friend, you must first be your own friend. By cultivating a healthy relationship with yourself, you are better equipped to foster meaningful connections and be authentic in your interactions with others.

Chapter 3

We Always Have a Choice

Making choices is a continuous journey of self-exploration and self-discipline. It is a process of achieving mastery over oneself.

Human existence is an intricate composition, the duality of our nature is akin to the two sides of a coin. Just as day is inseparable from night and truth coexists with lies, every individual possesses two distinct characters. The first character embodies intelligence, diligence, and a commitment to making sound decisions. This facet of our being consistently urges us to make the right choices. It acts as a guide, reminding us of what is truly beneficial and what is not. Even in the face of daunting challenges and obstacles that litter our path, this inner voice motivates us to tread on the righteous route towards our desired destination. It possesses a foresight that keenly considers the long-term consequences of the choices we make, ensuring our actions are in harmony with our future well-being.

On the other side, the second version of our character leans towards laziness and a penchant for seeking shortcuts. This aspect seeks the path of least resistance, regardless of its morality. It does not dwell on the potential ramifications of its choices, instead yearning for swift results by any means. This persona lacks the inclination to contemplate the consequences, focusing solely on achieving immediate outcomes whether through unethical shortcuts or a lack of consideration for ethical principles.

The unceasing battle between these two versions of ourselves shapes the choices we make and the trajectory of our lives. It is an ongoing battle between diligence and laziness, between ethical considerations and expediency. Each persona offers its own set of motivations and perspectives, presenting us with the choices that shape our lives and define our character.

Now it depends upon us to confront which side of our nature we want to embrace and allow to guide our actions. It is essential to recognize the influence of both aspects within us and allow us to consciously choose which voice to heed. The conscientious and industrious version of ourselves invites us to undertake the righteous path, paving the way for personal development and the realization of our goals. Simultaneously, succumbing to the allure of the indolent alter ego may lead us astray, lured by temptations of shortcuts and immediate gratification. However, the satisfaction derived from such expedient measures is often fleeting, leaving us vulnerable to the potential pitfalls that lie ahead.

In the pursuit of our goals and aspirations, it is essential to understand the significance of knowing the entire path to our destinations. While some may opt for shortcuts and dubious methods to reach their desired destination quickly, they may find themselves at a disadvantage if circumstances force them to start anew. Without the opportunity to rely on those questionable tactics again, the journey becomes exceedingly challenging to replicate.

Although choosing the honest and righteous path may initially seem slower, it offers invaluable benefits. By walking on the right path, we become intimately acquainted with the obstacles and challenges that lie ahead, allowing us to better prepare and navigate through them. Each step taken brings a deeper understanding of the trials encountered and the strategies required to overcome them. This acquired wisdom becomes a valuable asset if we find ourselves needing to undertake the journey again.

It may require additional time and effort to proceed honestly along the right path, the investment yields irreplaceable returns. Each hurdle becomes an opportunity for growth and learning, and the accumulated experience provides us with the confidence and capability to overcome future challenges.

I believe the most powerful weapon we possess is our own mind. It possesses remarkable capabilities that enable us to achieve great things and bring about positive change. On the other hand, if misused or directed in negative ways, the mind can also cause destruction and lead to adverse consequences.

Utilizing our minds in a constructive and positive manner leads us towards our dreams, the life that we have dreamt of, and fulfilling our aspirations. Our thoughts and mental abilities allow us to imagine, plan, innovate, and take actions towards our goals. Through focus, determination, and strategic thinking, we can overcome any obstacle, solve problems, and create meaningful outcomes.

Conversely, if we allow our minds to be consumed by negative thoughts, destructive behaviors, or harmful intentions, we risk losing all that we have built. If we use our minds in the wrong direction, we may engage in self-sabotaging behaviors or harm others. If our mind is misdirected, it can lead to regret, loss, and negative consequences.

This ability to utilize our minds for both positive and negative purposes sets humans apart from other species. While animals also require food to sustain themselves, humans possess the capacity for complex thinking and reasoning. We have the ability to make the conscious choices about what to eat, when to eat, and how to eat, based on our understanding of what is good or bad for our bodies.

As humans, we know the long-term consequences of our dietary choices. We can educate ourselves about the impact of different foods on our well-being and make informed decisions accordingly. Ultimately, what we eat today plays a significant role in shaping our future health. By making conscious decisions to nourish ourselves with nutritious and balanced meals, we can promote good health, prevent diseases, and enhance our overall quality of life.

People often express the opinion that there is a lack of positive or entertaining content in movies and television. However, the decision to watch television shows or movies is ultimately a matter of personal choice rather than compulsion. It is up to individuals to decide whether they want to engage in watching repetitive daily soaps with predictable storylines where people are getting married ten times, getting kidnapped twenty times, dying several times and then coming to existence again, God knows how and why? It is up to us to choose whether we want to watch explicit movies lacking substance, or opt for a content that expands their knowledge, evokes laughter, or genuinely touches their hearts.

While walking on the road, it is a common observation to see a significant number of people driving in the wrong direction. What is more concerning is that many individuals engage in this behavior with their entire families, including their children. When confronted about their actions, these individuals often respond with statements like

"Who has the time to take a long U-turn?"

"I am in a hurry; I am helpless", or

"What's your problem?"

Unfortunately, some encounters can escalate into fights or arguments.

It is important to note that driving in the wrong direction cannot be attributed to compulsion but rather personal choice. Those who choose to take their children on the wrong route fail to realize that their children are observing and learning from their actions. Consequently, there is a risk that these children will adopt the same behavior in the future, perpetuating not only a cycle of taking shortcuts on the road, but also to other areas of life as well, which will eventually have the risk of tragic injury.

Similarly, those who opt for the wrong direction to save time should consider the potential consequences. By taking such risks, they risk not reaching their destination at all, leaving their family waiting for an uncertain period.

Moreover, the repercussions of such choices extend beyond the individuals themselves. Innocent people who follow traffic rules and drive correctly are adversely affected by the actions of those who choose to drive the wrong way. It is essential for individuals to realize that their choices on the road have wider implications, affecting not only themselves but also those connected to them and at times some innocent strangers.

Certainly, the analogy of driving rules extends to our daily lives as well. Like if we drive with attentiveness, taking precautions such as wearing helmets, or seat belts, avoiding wrong paths, and refraining from driving too fast or recklessly, we can reach our desired destination without causing harm to others or ourselves. Similarly, by applying the principles of focus and concentration, taking necessary precautions, making informed choices, and avoiding impulsive or reckless behavior, we can navigate through life towards our desired goals and that too without causing harm to ourselves and others.

The essence of mentioning these examples is to highlight how the choices we make in our everyday lives can significantly impact our overall well-being and that of those around us.

I have read somewhere:

"Our choices should reflect hopes and happiness, not fear and compulsion"

This is exactly my point; our happiness and aspirations should stem from the choices we make, rather than being dictated by our fears and obligations. There are moments when we find ourselves in situations where we may not want to pursue a particular job or task, but we settle for it out of fear of the consequences to ourselves and our loved ones. Let's take the example of driving: many people wear helmets or seat belts primarily because they fear being fined, rather than truly prioritizing their own safety. However, the underlying motivation behind wearing helmets and seat belts should be our personal well-being.

Similarly, when it comes to any kind of work or job, our mindset should revolve around what we can do to improve our own lives and support our family, rather than just succumbing to fear and helplessness.

It's all about perspective.

Approaching the same task with a positive mindset can propel us to new heights and bring us a sense of fulfillment. Conversely, if we approach it with fear and a sense of helplessness, we will find ourselves stuck in a cycle of dissatisfaction and diminished confidence. This, in turn, hampers our ability to focus and demoralizes us. By embracing a positive outlook and taking ownership of our decisions, we can shape our lives in a way that brings us true satisfaction. Let your decisions be guided by hope, passion, and the belief that you can make a difference in your own life and the lives of those you care about.

When it comes to making the right choices in life, there is another perspective that should be considered:

"The past is the key to future."

Our journey through life consists of three interconnected phases: the past, the present, and the future. In this context, I believe that our past experiences play a crucial role in shaping our future. By reflecting on our previous choices, both good and bad, we can gather valuable insights that guide us towards making better choices today.

When we analyze our past decisions in the present moment, it allows us to understand the outcomes they have produced. We can examine the consequences of both good and bad choices and evaluate how they have influenced our lives. By doing so, we gain wisdom and knowledge that can help us navigate the path ahead.

It is essential for individuals to learn from the mistakes they have made in the past and try to consider different paths that could have been taken. Similarly, it is equally important to acknowledge the good choices we have made and recognize the positive outcomes they have brought.

Sometimes, people tend to believe that the consequences of their past wrong choices are unchangeable. While it is true that we cannot alter the past, it is crucial not to dwell on it solely in the present and harbor self-blame. Continuously blaming ourselves for past mistakes only jeopardizes our future. Instead, we should view those mistakes as valuable lessons. By internalizing the lessons learned and making a conscious effort to avoid repeating those errors, we set ourselves on a path of self-improvement and a more promising future.

The wrong decisions that currently weigh on our hearts, causing us to shed tears or feel sadness were once our present choices. Similarly, the choices we make today will become tomorrow's memories. Everything remains essentially the same — our essence, our minds — yet today we possess something additional, that is the accumulation of the outcomes of our past decisions, be they good or bad. These choices were absent in our lives at the time when we made them, but now they shape our experiences.

Perhaps this is why I often say that a person never truly loses anything; they always gain something. It ultimately depends on us whether we choose to embrace happiness or sorrow. Our present circumstances, our emotional state, and our future prospects are deeply influenced by the decisions we made in our past. In the journey of life, we are the driver of our own vehicle, and we have the ability to alter its direction and condition at any given moment.

Numerous articles and books delve into the complexities of decision-making, offering various factors, methodologies, processes, and strategies to enhance our choices. They may have the ability to refine our choices, however, in my view, one effortless formula is based on one simple fundamental principle. As I mentioned earlier, we possess two distinct characteristics within us: one characterized by hard work and strong ethical values, and the other tempted by shortcuts and influenced by worldly affairs.

When faced with a choice, I firmly believe the key is to listen to the voice from within and follow the very first instinct. The very first instinct that arises within us is often a reflection of our genuine self – the version driven by values. By heeding this initial voice, you can make the right choice. I assure you that you will never regret it, as the initial instinct is a true representation of our authentic self, our original version.

Opting to embrace happiness, generosity, kindness, forgiveness, and helpfulness can bring about profound transformations within oneself. By consciously making these choices, we uplift and enhance our character as a person.

Choosing happiness allows us to find joy and contentment amidst life's challenges

Embracing a giving nature enables us to make a positive impact on the lives of others.

Cultivating kindness fosters compassion and empathy.

Practicing forgiveness grants us the freedom to let go of resentment and find inner peace.

Being helpful allows us to extend a helping hand and support those in need.

These choices not only uplift us but also create a ripple effect, spreading positivity and making the world a better place.

Chapter 4

Satisfaction over Success

In today's world, it is common for people to be easily influenced by others and worldly affairs. It is human nature to aspire for success, wealth, and recognition, and often, we find ourselves looking up to individuals who possess these attributes. We are drawn to their achievements, their lavish lifestyles, and their elevated social status, yearning to emulate their paths to success. However, it is crucial to recognize that those we admire have traversed their unique journeys to attain their own current positions.

When we fixate solely on the external markers of success displayed by these individuals, we may inadvertently undermine the progress we have made in our own lives. It is easy to overlook the years of hard work, dedication, failures, and lessons they have experienced along the way. By attempting to replicate their current state without understanding the path they have followed, we risk jeopardizing our own personal growth and accomplishments.

Instead of fixating on what others have achieved, it is more productive to focus on self-reflection and introspection. By understanding our own aspirations, talents, and interests, we can set meaningful and authentic goals that are tailored to our individual paths. This allows us to cultivate our own sense of purpose and create a life that is fulfilling and true to ourselves.

While it is natural to seek inspiration from successful individuals, it is important to maintain a healthy perspective. We should admire their accomplishments while recognizing that our own journeys are distinct. By embracing our uniqueness, leveraging our strengths, and learning from both successes and failures, we can forge a path that is genuinely ours.

In today's fast-paced and interconnected world, it has become increasingly easy to get influenced by others, particularly with the rise of social media and the phenomenon of "influencers." However, I firmly believe that instead of succumbing to external influences, we should seek inspiration from others while staying true to our own authentic selves. The danger of being influenced lies in the potential loss of our authenticity and originality. When we constantly strive to imitate others, we risk diluting our own unique perspectives, talents, and values. This can lead to a sense of disconnection from our true selves and an inability to fully express our genuine desires and aspirations.

While success is often equated with external markers such as wealth, fame, or societal recognition, true satisfaction can only be attained by embracing our authenticity and genuineness. It is important to recognize that success attained through imitation may not necessarily bring lasting fulfillment. In fact, chasing someone else's version of success often leaves us feeling unfulfilled and disconnected from our own purpose.

By prioritizing authenticity, we tap into the wellspring of our individuality and personal growth. Embracing our unique identities and staying true to our values allows us to cultivate a deep sense of satisfaction that transcends societal expectations and external validation. When we live authentically, we build genuine connections with others, as our true selves naturally attract those who appreciate and resonate with our authentic expression.

However, nurturing authenticity in a world driven by influencers and external pressures requires conscious effort. It involves self-reflection, introspection, and a willingness to detach ourselves from the constant comparison with others. We can start by examining our own values, passions, and aspirations, and aligning our actions with what truly matters to us. Surrounding ourselves with positive role models who inspire us rather than influence us can also help shape our path towards satisfaction.

It is crucial to redefine our understanding of success and prioritize satisfaction over external measures. Authentic success encompasses not only professional achievements but also personal growth, meaningful relationships, self-acceptance, and well-being. By focusing on our individual journey and nurturing our unique talents and passions, we can create a life that is genuinely satisfying and aligned with our true selves.

Getting inspired by someone goes beyond merely observing their current achievements or possessions. It involves delving into their journey, understanding their struggles, failures, and the lessons they have learned along the way.

When we seek inspiration, we acknowledge and appreciate the path that others have walked. We recognize the hard work, perseverance, and resilience they have demonstrated to overcome obstacles and achieve their goals. By understanding their experiences, we gain valuable insights that we can apply to our own lives, considering our unique circumstances and aspirations.

In contrast, getting influenced by someone often focuses solely on their present achievements or material possessions. There is little emphasis on understanding the process or the values that underpin their success. This approach can lead to a shallow imitation of their external circumstances without truly comprehending the journey that led them there.

To truly benefit from others' experiences, it is essential to go beyond surface-level observation and delve into the underlying principles and strategies that guided them. By studying their failures, setbacks, and growth, we gain a more comprehensive understanding of the challenges they faced and the choices they made to overcome them.

Applying their insights and lessons to our own lives requires adaptability. We must assess how we can incorporate their wisdom into our unique circumstances, taking into account our own strengths, weaknesses, and aspirations. It's about learning from their experiences, extracting the underlying principles, and applying them in a way that aligns with our individual paths.

By seeking inspiration rather than mere influence, we can tap into the rich tapestry of human experiences, gaining wisdom that transcends superficial success and material achievements.

In our society, success and satisfaction are often considered synonymous, with the assumption that achieving success will automatically lead to a sense of satisfaction. However, it is important to recognize that success and satisfaction are distinct concepts each with its own implications and measurements.

Success is often perceived as an external validation, commonly measured by others, societal standards and materialistic achievements. It is influenced by how others perceive our accomplishments and is often associated with tangible rewards such as wealth, status, or recognition. The pursuit of success can be driven by societal expectations and comparisons, leading individuals to prioritize external achievements over personal fulfillment.

On the other hand, satisfaction is an inwardly-directed evaluation of our own well-being and contentment. It is a subjective measure that stems from aligning our actions and choices with our inner values and aspirations. Satisfaction is deeply connected to our inner selves, our passions, and our sense of purpose. It encompasses a sense of fulfillment, peace, and joy that arises from living in alignment with our authentic selves.

Let's think about it this way: in every person's life, there is at least one hobby that acts as a magical escape, allowing them to momentarily forget all their troubles. This enchanting effect occurs because they pour their heart into this activity, caring little about their proficiency or the opinions of others.

Consider the vast array of passions people have–some are captivated by singing, losing themselves in the melody, others find solace in painting, bringing their imagination to life on canvas. Some discover joy in the culinary arts, creating dishes that delight the senses, while others are drawn to the water, feeling liberated as they swim. Then there are those who find their sanctuary in writing, weaving words into stories that transport them to another world.

When someone pursues an activity with genuine enthusiasm and no ulterior motives, they gradually become skilled at it. But more than the skill, it's the profound sense of fulfillment and happiness that makes it truly special. This is why having a hobby is essential–it nourishes the soul and brings joy to life.

However, it's important to ensure that our hobbies do not cause harm to others or society. While a hobby can bring immense personal joy, it should not come at the expense of someone else's well-being. True satisfaction comes from knowing that your passion is a source of positivity and not a cause of distress. So cherish your hobbies, pursue them with all your heart, but always be mindful of their impact on the world around you.

It is crucial to reflect on and ask ourselves whether we are truly successful or satisfied. Success without genuine satisfaction can feel empty and unfulfilling, as it may be driven by external validation and the pursuit of societal expectations. It may lead to a relentless pursuit of material gains at the expense of personal well-being, relationships, and a sense of purpose. In contrast, when we prioritize satisfaction, we focus on inner growth, self-awareness, and nurturing our passions and values. This path encourages a more holistic and balanced approach to life, where external achievements are seen as complementary to our internal state of contentment.

While it is important to strive for both success and satisfaction, it is crucial to recognize that success without satisfaction can be detrimental. A single-minded pursuit of success may lead to selfishness, as the focus is primarily on personal gains and external validation. In contrast, satisfaction embodies a more giving nature, as it involves aligning our actions with our values and making a positive impact on ourselves and others.

In today's digital age, social media platforms provide us with glimpses into the lives of celebrities and influencers, often leaving us impressed and fascinated by their seemingly successful lifestyles.

The rapid growth of social media has made it possible for individuals to attain overnight fame and become influencers themselves. However, it is essential to go beyond the surface-level admiration and question what truly makes them successful.

Success, in its simplest form, can be achieved through various means, especially with the accessibility and reach offered by social media. But it is crucial to consider the impact that success is creating. Merely attaining success without considering its consequences or the impact on the world can be shortsighted. It is important to evaluate whether our success contributes positively to society, promotes values we believe in, and leaves a lasting impact on others.

Furthermore, success should not be measured solely by external validation or the admiration of others. It is equally important to consider the respect and dignity we earn through our achievements. Building a reputation based on integrity, ethical conduct, and positive contributions adds depth and meaning to success. True success goes beyond material possessions and public recognition; it encompasses the respect and esteem we garner from our actions and the positive impact we create. While external achievements and societal recognition may provide a temporary sense of fulfillment, true satisfaction comes from aligning our actions with our values, passions, and personal aspirations.

Success is not an overnight achievement but a result of a long and arduous journey filled with hard work, sacrifices, determination, discipline, and perseverance. It requires consistent effort, often accompanied by numerous sleepless nights and countless ups and downs. When success is attained through such a process, it becomes more meaningful and enduring, leading to a deeper sense of satisfaction.

On the other hand, success that is achieved overnight or through shortcuts often lacks the foundation and depth necessary for long-term sustainability. Such fleeting success can bring temporary happiness and a sense of accomplishment, but it is prone to vanish just as quickly as it appeared. Those who experience instant success without going through the necessary challenges may struggle to maintain their newfound status and may find it difficult to navigate the complexities that come with it. This can lead to a lack of fulfillment and an inability to sustain relationships and other aspects of life.

In contrast, success that is earned through genuine effort and authenticity leads to a deeper sense of fulfillment and satisfaction. When we invest our time, energy, and passion into a meaningful endeavor, the resulting success carries more significance and lasting value. It is through the challenges and setbacks we encounter along the way that we develop resilience and acquire the skills necessary to maintain and build upon our achievements.

It's important to recognize that temporary happiness, joy, and even relationships can be associated with superficial success. When success is solely based on external factors, it becomes transient and vulnerable to changing circumstances.

The saying "Everyone salutes the rising sun" highlights the common phenomenon of people acknowledging and celebrating success without necessarily understanding the journey and efforts behind it. As time passes, circumstances can change, and the admiration and recognition received may fluctuate. It emphasizes the importance of recognizing that success achieved through genuine and authentic efforts is more likely to lead to lasting happiness and authentic relationships.

It is rooted in the values, integrity, and purpose that drive our actions. Genuine success not only brings personal happiness but also cultivates authentic relationships with others. It attracts like-minded individuals who appreciate and respect the journey and efforts undertaken, leading to more meaningful connections and sustainable support networks.

Success is often defined as the achievement of one's goals, and these goals can vary greatly from person to person. Society often associates success with tangible outcomes such as earning money, acquiring assets, or gaining fame. However, it is important to recognize that success is not solely defined by these external markers.

True success goes beyond mere achievement and encompasses a deeper sense of satisfaction and fulfillment.

Using the analogy of hunger, if our goal is simply to fill our stomach, any food may suffice. However, true satisfaction comes from choosing and enjoying a meal that aligns with our personal preferences, nourishes our body and soul, and provides a sense of fulfillment beyond mere satiation. In this example, satisfaction represents the deeper level of contentment and happiness that arises from fulfilling our desires and personal preferences.

Similarly, in the pursuit of success, it is crucial to prioritize satisfaction. This means setting goals that align with our values, passions, and aspirations, and working towards them in a way that brings us joy and fulfillment. It involves finding meaning and purpose in our actions, rather than solely focusing on external achievements.

Ultimately, success and satisfaction go hand in hand. While success may involve the accomplishment of goals, it is the accompanying sense of satisfaction that truly completes the picture.

If success is solely defined by material wealth, then individuals who engage in illegal activities or fraudulent behavior could be considered successful. However, it is important to note that true success encompasses more than just monetary gain or fame.

Success should not be measured solely by external factors, but also by the integrity of our actions and the impact we have on others and society. Respect and moral values play a significant role in determining the true measure of success. It is through genuine satisfaction and a sense of fulfillment that we can attain respect from others and build meaningful relationships.

Robbers, fraudsters, or individuals who achieve fame through unethical means may have material wealth or notoriety, but they often lack the respect and genuine satisfaction that comes from acting with integrity and making positive contributions to society. Their success may be temporary and fleeting, as it is not built on a foundation of honesty and ethical behavior.

In contrast, true success is achieved when we pursue our goals and aspirations in a way that aligns with our values and principles. It involves making choices and taking actions that are not only beneficial to ourselves but also considerate of others. By acting with integrity, honesty, and empathy, we earn the respect and admiration of others.

Success is not a static or final destination but rather an ongoing journey that evolves over time. It is influenced by various factors such as circumstances, age, and specific situations. What may be considered success in one stage of life or within a particular context may not hold the same significance in another.

During childhood, success may be associated with achievements such as coming first in class or winning a medal in a race. In the college years, success could be obtaining a scholarship or receiving recognition for academic accomplishments. In the professional realm, success may be measured by meeting targets, receiving promotions, receiving salary hikes, or earning awards.

As we grow and evolve, our definitions and expectations of success also change. What we consider to be a significant accomplishment at one point in our lives may not carry the same weight as we mature and experience new things. Our understanding of success becomes more nuanced and multifaceted.

Furthermore, success is subjective and personal. It is important to recognize that success can take different forms for different people. It could be pursuing a passion, maintaining a healthy work-life balance, nurturing relationships, making a positive impact on others, or achieving personal growth and self-fulfillment.

The meaning of success can also fluctuate throughout our lives. As we reach certain milestones or accomplish specific goals, our aspirations and desires may change. We may set new objectives and strive for different forms of success. It is important to embrace the evolving nature of success and adapt our perspectives accordingly.

While determination and focus are valuable qualities in achieving our goals, it is crucial to maintain a balanced approach that considers the impact on our personal lives and relationships.

In the pursuit of success, individuals often dedicate significant time and effort towards their goals. This can mean working long hours, sacrificing personal time, and neglecting other areas of life such as family, relationships, hobbies, and self-care. While this level of dedication can lead to short-term gains, it can also have long-term consequences on our overall well-being and satisfaction.

Neglecting the people and things around us in the pursuit of success can have negative consequences. It may strain relationships, lead to feelings of isolation, and contribute to a sense of emptiness, even if external achievements are attained. A healthy and fulfilling life encompasses not only professional success but also nurturing meaningful connections, maintaining physical and mental well-being, and finding joy in everyday experiences.

Moreover, success should not be seen as an endpoint or a destination that, once reached, guarantees eternal satisfaction. The journey towards success is ongoing and ever-evolving. Setting new goals, striving for continuous growth, and adapting to changing circumstances are integral parts of the process.

It is essential to strike a balance between ambition and personal well-being. This involves setting realistic expectations, setting boundaries, and recognizing the importance of self-care, rest, and meaningful connections with others. By nurturing our personal lives alongside our professional aspirations, we can create a more sustainable and fulfilling path to success.

For many individuals, success includes providing a comfortable and secure life for their family, which often involves financial stability. Working hard and striving for financial growth are indeed important aspects of achieving this goal. However, it is equally vital to recognize that success extends beyond monetary achievements.

Success also involves being present for our loved ones. It means being available when they need us, spending quality time with them, and nurturing those relationships. True success encompasses the ability to strike a balance between work and personal life, juggling the demands of work and family without dropping the balls.

Maintaining this balance can be challenging, as it requires conscious effort and prioritization. By actively working on achieving this balance, we can create a fulfilling and well-rounded life.

According to my opinion, striving to be an inspirer rather than an influencer is a valuable mindset. Being an inspirer means leading by example, motivating and supporting others through our actions, achievements, and character. It involves positively impacting those around us and encouraging them to pursue their own goals and aspirations.

On the other hand, being an influencer can sometimes be associated with superficiality and a focus on external appearances rather than genuine inspiration. By being an inspirer, we can contribute to the growth and success of others in a more meaningful and impactful way.

Maintaining a balance between personal and professional life, prioritizing the happiness of our loved ones, and being an inspiration are important principles to cultivate for a well-rounded and fulfilling life.

Chapter 5

Be a Fighter

In the tapestry of human existence, there exists an underlying truth that transcends mere survival - the essence of being a fighter. It's a notion often whispered in the corridors of adversity, a mantra echoing through the annals of time, a testament to the resilience ingrained within the human spirit. For me, it's not just a fleeting sentiment; it's a fundamental belief, a guiding principle that shapes the contours of my worldview.

Picture this: a vast expanse of life's canvas stretching before us, brimming with endless possibilities, each stroke laden with the promise of triumph or tribulation. Amidst this cosmic theater, I often find myself urging others to embrace the mantle of a fighter. But what does it truly mean to be a fighter? Is it merely a label reserved for those who wield physical prowess in the arena of combat? Or does it delve deeper, touching the very core of our being?

In my reflections, I've come to understand that being a fighter transcends the confines of brute strength or martial skill. It's a multifaceted tapestry woven with threads of resilience, determination, and unwavering resolve. When I speak about being a fighter, I'm not just referring to the physical combat you might see in sports like boxing or wrestling. Yes, physical prowess may play a part, but the true essence of a fighter lies in the battleground of the mind, the arena where our deepest fears and insecurities clash with the beacon of hope.

Consider the warrior who stands not just against external adversaries but grapples with the tempest raging within – battling doubts, wrestling with uncertainties, and confronting the shadows that lurk in the recesses of the soul. This, I believe, is the hallmark of a true fighter – the ability to wage war on multiple fronts, confronting not just the external foes but the inner demons that threaten to ensnare us.

I recall a time when I witnessed someone close to me fight a battle of this kind. A dear friend of mine was going through a particularly difficult period in his life. On the surface, he appeared to have it all together–successful career, supportive family, and a seemingly unshakeable resolve. But beneath that strong exterior, he was wrestling with deep-seated insecurities and a growing sense of self-doubt.

He confided in me one evening, his voice carrying the weight of someone who had been silently fighting for far too long. The pressures of work, the fear of not being enough, and the relentless pursuit of perfection had taken their toll. He spoke of sleepless nights filled with anxious thoughts, moments where he felt paralyzed by the fear of failure, and days where even getting out of bed seemed like a monumental task.

What struck me most was not just the intensity of his struggle, but his courage to face it head-on. Rather than letting these inner demons consume him, he chose to confront them. He sought help, started opening up about his struggles, and began the difficult journey of understanding and healing. It wasn't an easy path, and there were setbacks along the way, but his determination to reclaim his life was nothing short of inspiring.

Witnessing his battle against his inner demons taught me that true strength is not just about overcoming external challenges but about having the courage to face the battles within. It reminded me that we all carry burdens, often hidden from the world, and that the bravest among us are those who dare to confront them.

Yet, it doesn't end there. A fighter's battlefield extends beyond the realms of the mind, encompassing the turbulent seas of emotion and the labyrinthine corridors of the heart. How often do we find ourselves embroiled in the throes of emotional turmoil, grappling with the tumultuous currents of joy, sorrow, anger, and despair? In these moments, it is the fighter within us that rises to the fore, navigating the turbulent waters with steadfast resolve.

And then there's the most clandestine battle of all – the silent struggle against our own happiness. How paradoxical it seems, to fight against the very thing we yearn for! Yet, such is the nature of the human condition, fraught with contradictions and enigmas. It is here, in the quiet recesses of our being, that the true test of resilience unfolds – the ability to embrace happiness amidst the chaos, to find solace in the midst of strife.

I firmly believe that each and every one of us is a fighter in our own right. From the quiet strength of a mother battling adversity to provide for her children, to the indomitable spirit of an artist pouring their soul onto the canvas, we are all warriors on the journey of life, navigating the twists and turns with courage and conviction.

In the realm of combat, there exist two distinct arenas: the structured environment of combat sports and the raw reality of real-life fights that unfold on the streets or elsewhere. While both involve physical confrontation, the disparities between the two are stark and consequential.

In combat sports such as boxing, karate, kabaddi, wrestling, and various other forms, fighters enter the ring or arena with a clear objective. Here, the stakes are high, but the rules are well-defined. Competitors vie for victory, not only for personal glory but also for the tangible rewards that accompany success.

In this domain, fighters have the opportunity to earn money, gain fame, and carve out a name for themselves in the annals of history. Their feats of strength and skill are celebrated, and they receive accolades from fans and admirers. It's a world where dedication and discipline are revered, where years of hard work and practice culminate in moments of triumph.

On the other hand, real-life fights, often unfolding in the unscripted chaos of the streets, present a starkly different reality. Here, the consequences of physical confrontation are far more severe, and the risks are amplified. Engaging in altercations outside the confines of a controlled environment can have life-altering repercussions, both legally and socially.

In these situations, individuals involved in physical altercations may find themselves entangled in a web of legal consequences. Assault charges, legal fees, and potential imprisonment loom ominously, casting a shadow over the impulsive actions of the moment. Moreover, the fallout from such encounters can tarnish one's reputation, branding them as a troublemaker or thug in the eyes of society.

The stark disparity between the outcomes of combat sports and real-life fights can be attributed to several factors, chief among them being the level of skill and preparation involved. In combat sports, fighters undergo rigorous training regimens, honing their skills over years of dedicated practice. They learn the intricacies of their chosen discipline, master techniques, and develop strategies to outmaneuver opponents. Moreover, they compete within the confines of established rules and regulations, ensuring a level playing field and a fair contest.

In contrast, real-life fights are often characterized by impulsivity, lack of training, and a disregard for consequences. Individuals involved in such altercations may act on impulse, driven by anger, fear, or other intense emotions. Without the discipline and training of professional fighters, they are ill-equipped to handle the physical and psychological demands of combat. As a result, these encounters often descend into chaos, with unpredictable outcomes and far-reaching repercussions.

Within the confines of the ring, where combatants clash in a flurry of blows and maneuvers, victory and defeat hang in delicate balance. Yet, it is not the outcome alone that defines the true essence of a fighter, but rather how they respond; not in the glory of triumph, but in the humility of defeat.

When two adversaries' step into the ring, they do so with the understanding that only one will emerge victorious. Yet, regardless of the outcome, the mark of a true fighter lies in their response to both victory and defeat. For them, each bout is an opportunity for growth, a chance to hone their skills and refine their craft.

In victory, the true fighter does not bask in the glow of success or revel in the adulation of the crowd. Instead, they humbly acknowledge the role of their mentors, coaches, and training partners who have supported them on their journey. They reflect on the strategies and techniques that led to their triumph, recognizing that every move, every decision played a part in their success. And most crucially, they guard against complacency, knowing that the path to greatness is paved with humility and hard work.

Similarly, in defeat, the true fighter does not wallow in self-pity or succumb to despair. Instead, they display grace and sportsmanship, acknowledging the skill and prowess of their opponent. They embrace defeat not as a setback, but as an opportunity for introspection and growth. They analyze their performance with a critical eye, identifying areas for improvement and learning from their mistakes. And with each defeat, they emerge stronger, wiser, and more determined to succeed.

In many ways, life itself mirrors the dynamics of the fighting ring, presenting us with challenges and opportunities within the bounds of its constraints. Just as combatants must navigate the confines of the ring, so too must we navigate the boundaries and limitations of our own existence. Within these parameters, we are called upon to perform our duties, pursue our aspirations, and confront the myriad trials that lie in wait.

Yet, like the fighter in the ring, we are not defined by the outcome of our endeavors but by the manner in which we face them. Whether we emerge victorious or taste the bitterness of defeat, our response to adversity speaks volumes about our character and resilience. Like a fighter in the ring, we must approach life's challenges with humility, determination, and a steadfast commitment to self-improvement.

Before stepping into the ring, fighters undergo rigorous training and are briefed on the rules of engagement to ensure a fair and safe contest. These rules serve as guidelines, ensuring that both competitors can showcase their skills without risking injury to themselves or their opponent. During the fight, any deviation from these rules results in warnings, with repeated infractions leading to disqualification.

Similarly, as we embark on our life's journey, we are taught the fundamental principles and values that guide us in navigating life's challenges and opportunities. Whether it's our parents, teachers, or mentors, each plays a crucial role in imparting these essential lessons. These rules serve as the moral compass that guides our actions and decisions. Just as breaking the rules in the ring results in warnings and penalties, so too do our actions in real life have consequences. Every misstep, every transgression, carries with it the risk of setback or defeat. And just like in the ring, the severity of the punishment often corresponds to the gravity of the offense.

Yet, just as the ring offers fighters the opportunity to learn from their mistakes and redeem themselves in subsequent rounds. So, too, does life afford us chances for growth and redemption. Each setback and each failure is an opportunity to reflect, learn, and improve. By acknowledging our mistakes, embracing humility, and making a commitment to change, we can chart a course towards personal growth and success.

Just as a coach guides and mentors a fighter in the ring, life itself serves as the ultimate coach on our journey. It imparts invaluable lessons and wisdom, shaping our understanding of the world and ourselves. We've all heard the adage, "Never accept defeat," and while perseverance is undoubtedly important, it's also crucial to recognize when our efforts are not yielding the desired results.

In life, setbacks and disappointments are inevitable, but they can also serve as powerful trigger for growth and self-improvement. When faced with obstacles or failures, it's essential to pause and reflect on our actions and decisions. Rather than stubbornly persisting in our current approach, we must be willing to reassess our strategies and make necessary adjustments.

Acknowledging our mistakes and shortcomings is not a sign of weakness but a testament to our willingness to grow and evolve. Often, individuals may believe they've followed the right path, yet find themselves falling short of their goals. In such instances, it's imperative to adopt a new perspective, to explore alternative strategies, and to be open to change.

However, embracing change can be daunting for many. It requires a willingness to step outside of one's comfort zone, to challenge established beliefs and assumptions. Yet, it is through this process of adaptation and transformation that true growth occurs. By recognizing the need for change and taking proactive steps to course-correct, we can break free from the cycle of repeating past mistakes and chart a new trajectory towards success.

Life's lessons are not always easy or straightforward. They often come in the form of adversity, setbacks, and challenges. Yet, it is precisely through these trials that we gain the wisdom and resilience to navigate life's complexities. As we confront our failures with courage and humility, we emerge stronger, wiser, and better equipped to face whatever obstacles lie ahead.

A skilled fighter knows that success in the ring begins with a thorough assessment of their opponent. They meticulously study their rival, analyzing their strengths and weaknesses, to devise a strategy that maximizes their chances of victory. Similarly, in the arena of life, it's imperative to recognize our own adversaries – and often, the most formidable opponent we face is none other than ourselves.

Understanding ourselves is the first step towards achieving success and fulfillment in life. Just as a fighter must assess their opponent's capabilities, we must take stock of our own strengths and weaknesses. This introspective process allows us to identify areas where we excel and areas where we need improvement, empowering us to chart a course towards personal growth and achievement.

Success is a deeply personal concept, unique to each individual. For some, it may be measured in professional accomplishments or material wealth, while for others, it may be found in personal relationships, creative pursuits, or inner peace. Yet, regardless of our aspirations, the journey towards success begins with self-awareness.

By understanding our strengths, we can leverage them to our advantage, capitalizing on our talents and abilities to pursue our goals with confidence and determination. Conversely, by acknowledging our weaknesses, we can take proactive steps to address them, whether through education, training, or seeking support from others.

Moreover, self-awareness empowers us to set meaningful goals that align with our authentic selves, rather than succumbing to external pressures or societal expectations. When we understand who we are and what we truly value, we can chart a course for success that is both fulfilling and sustainable.

In the ring, every match is overseen by a referee whose watchful gaze ensures fairness and upholds the rules of combat. Similarly, in the vast arena of life, there exists a divine referee—the omnipresent and omniscient God—who observes every action, thought, and intention with unwavering vigilance. While it may sometimes seem that unethical actions go unnoticed or even lead to temporary gains, it is essential to recognize that God's watchful eyes never waver, and His justice is absolute.

Indeed, there are moments in life when one may be tempted to stray from the path of righteousness, enticed by the allure of immediate gratification or worldly success. However, it is crucial to remember that true victory is not measured by fleeting triumphs obtained through deceit or wrongdoing. Just as a fighter may win a few rounds through underhanded tactics, the ultimate prize—the respect of one's peers, the satisfaction of a clear conscience, and the favor of the divine—is reserved for those who uphold integrity and honor.

For every action, there is a consequence, and every choice carries weight in the eyes of God. While the allure of short-term gains may be enticing, the price of compromising one's principles far outweighs any temporary benefits. In the cosmic arena of life, cheating may grant momentary advantages, but it inevitably leads to a loss of integrity, self-respect, and ultimately, spiritual fulfillment.

In contrast, those who embrace the path of righteousness, who strive to become true fighters in the arena of life, are richly rewarded in ways that transcend material success. By adhering to principles of honesty, compassion, and moral integrity, individuals align themselves with the divine will and open themselves to blessings beyond measure.

Moreover, the belief in divine justice offers solace to those who have been wronged or marginalized, comforting them that their suffering will not go unnoticed or unaddressed. In the cosmic arena of life, every action carries consequences, and every individual has the opportunity to rectify their mistakes and strive for redemption.

To be a true fighter in life, one should align his actions with the higher purpose of righteousness and virtue, knowing that in the end, it is not earthly accolades or material wealth that define our worth, but the content of our character and the integrity of our soul.

Chapter 6

God is Not Listening to Me

At times, it is common for us to experience moments of doubt and frustration when we feel that our prayers and pleas to God are going unheard or unanswered. This feeling often arises when faced with challenging circumstances, such as difficulties in various aspects of life, and we seek divine intervention to bring about a positive change or resolution.

Many times, I hear this from friends and known ones that they are going through a very rough patch in life, or they are really tense about their job or business. They have family problems, or they are not in good terms with their partner/spouse, and that they are praying to God to bring them out of that worse situation and resolve their issues, but God is not listening to them.

During such moments, it is common to question whether God is truly listening and responding to our struggles.

The belief that God does not listen to us is subjective and can vary from person to person. However, I believe that God always listens to our prayers and pleas, regardless of the circumstances we find ourselves in. It is important to recognize that our relationship with God is multifaceted, akin to other relationships we have in our lives.

I believe that God is omnipresent, all-knowing, and compassionate.

Like any relationship, our connection with God is built on trust, belief, fear, respect, and faith. We trust that God is watching over us, caring for us, and guiding us through life's challenges. We believe in a higher power that listens to our prayers and has the ability to bring out positive change. There may be a sense of fear and reverence, acknowledging the divine presence and power.

However, just like in any other relationship, communication is the key. It is through prayer, meditation, and spiritual practices that we engage in a dialogue with God. We express our hopes, fears, desires, and concerns by laying our thoughts and feelings before the Almighty. This two-way communication fosters a deeper connection and strengthens our relationship with God.

During good times, it's easy to unintentionally neglect our communication with God. We may become complacent or take our blessings for granted. We may stop seeking guidance, expressing gratitude, or finding solace in prayers. This lack of communication can lead to a perceived distance or the feeling that God is not listening. However, it is important to remember that our relationship with God is not solely dependent on our needs or hardships. It's a continuous journey of connection, even during times of abundance and joy.

When we actively communicate with God, whether through prayer, meditation, or reflection, we nurture the bond and strengthen our connection. Following this practice, we can experience a deeper sense of trust, belief, and understanding in our relationship with the divine. Just like any other relationship, maintaining a two-way communication with God helps foster a sense of intimacy and connection. It allows us to share our feelings, knowing that we are being heard or understood. It is through this active engagement that we can experience the comfort, guidance, and support that we seek from a higher power.

"God's attentiveness to our prayers and needs is rooted in the understanding of God's compassionate nature."

To illustrate it, let's take an example of friendship:

It is a valuable relationship built on trust, support, and mutual understanding. In a healthy friendship, communication and interaction should go both ways, with both parties actively engaging and showing interest in each other's lives. However, if one friend only reaches out when they need something or when they are in trouble, after a period of time, it can lead to feelings of disappointment, frustration, and even resentment. This kind of behavior can create an imbalance in the friendship, as it may give the impression that the friend is only interested in their own needs and not in maintaining a genuine connection.

In such situations, you may begin to question the sincerity and authenticity of the friendship and feel that it is one-sided, that they are being selfish or self-centered. It is natural to expect reciprocity and a sense of mutuality in a healthy friendship, where both parties contribute to the relationship and offer love, support, and kindness when needed.

The same principle applies to our relationship with God. Just like a friendship, it thrives on ongoing communication, trust, and appreciation. It is important to recognize and acknowledge God's presence and blessings in our lives consistently. We should stop approaching God solely in times of trouble, we should cultivate a genuine and selfless connection with God, where we approach him not only when we need something but also in moments of joy, reflection, and gratitude. We should engage ourselves in daily conversations with God, just to thank Him for the blessings He has provided and talk to Him about various aspects of life like we do with our friends. We should treat God as a trusted friend, someone with whom we can share our hopes, dreams, fears, and challenges. Believe me, it helps in creating a sense of closeness and understanding.

When we establish this kind of connection with God, we come to understand that He is always listening and caring, and He is there for us all the time, regardless of whether we are facing hardships or enjoying a period of prosperity.

By talking to God selflessly, without any specific wish or request, we shift the focus of our relationship from seeking personal gain to building a genuine connection based on love, trust, and appreciation.

Life is indeed a journey filled with a multitude of experiences, both joyful and challenging. It is during these ups and downs that we may pause and reflect on the support and care we receive, and it is often in these moments that we realize the presence of God in our lives.

Happiness and sorrow often go hand in hand. We appreciate happiness more deeply because we have experienced sorrow, and sorrow often allows us to grow and appreciate the value of joy. Similarly, laughter and tears are intertwined. Laughter brings lightness and joy to our lives, while tears provide an outlet for our emotions and help us heal.

Just as there are golden days filled with success, love, and fulfillment, there will also be dark days when we face challenges, setbacks, or losses. These contrasting experiences shape us and contribute to our growth as individuals. They teach us resilience, empathy, and the capacity to appreciate the good times even more.

The beauty of life lies in its inherent contrast. Without the lows, we wouldn't fully appreciate the highs. The challenges we encounter provide opportunities for personal development, learning, and self-discovery. They test our strength and resilience, allowing us to emerge stronger and wiser.

It is important to remember that life is not a linear path; it is a series of peaks and valleys. The ups and downs serve as a reminder that change is constant and that we have the capacity to navigate through both triumphs and tribulations.

However, have you ever realized that despite so many ups and downs in our lives, from childhood until whatever age we are now?

Who is supporting us?

Who is taking care of us?

Who is always there for us?

Who is the reason for our survival for so many years?

It is God, the supreme power, who is with us all the time.

From the very beginning of our existence, God has been our constant companion. He is the one who supports us, takes care of us, and remains by our side when others may come and go. When we take a moment to acknowledge the presence of God in our lives, we start to recognize the countless blessings and provisions that have been bestowed upon us. It is through his grace and mercy that we have thrived for so many years. God's love and protection are unwavering, even in the darkest moments we may feel alone or abandoned.

By engaging in conversations with God, talking to Him selflessly, without any specific expectations, we open ourselves up to receiving His boundless blessings. When we talk to God with humility and open heart, we tap into His limitless love and compassion. His blessings may transcend our expectations and go beyond what we could have imagined. Following this practice, we allow Him to work in mysterious and wondrous ways, guiding us towards paths of peace, contentment, and fulfillment.

One humble piece of advice:

"Just talk to God without expectations, and He will give you something beyond your imagination."

This is not restricted to God alone; this phenomenon applies to every relationship. Just be selfless.

Chapter 7

Life is a Beautiful Gift

When it comes to the question of "How to live life?"

It is a deeply personal and subjective experience, and there are no one-size-fits-all answers. Everyone's journey is unique, and the approach to life can vary greatly depending on individual circumstances, values, and aspirations.

I am eager to express and share my personal perspective and insights regarding the same question "How to live life?" I believe it is important to engage in a thoughtful exploration and exchange of ideas surrounding us in order to gain a deeper understanding. By expressing my views, I hope to contribute to a meaningful dialogue that encourages introspection and offers different perspectives on the diverse approaches individuals may consider while navigating through life's complexities. My ambition is to foster a space where others can reflect, challenge, and contribute their own viewpoints, ultimately enriching our collective understanding of the various ways to approach and experience life.

In my opinion, there can be two approaches to life:

1. Birth-Struggle-Death:

Here, we acknowledge the presence of struggle as an integral part of life. This approach may lead to personal growth and the development of inner strength, but it can sometimes result in a mindset that is constantly focused on overcoming challenges, potentially causing individuals to overlook or neglect other aspects of life, such as relationships and personal well-being.

2. Birth (relationships, love, success, failure, achievements, joy, happiness, and feelings) and the end of a beautiful journey:

Here, the emphasis is on the significance of relationships, love, enjoyment, and personal growth throughout one's journey. It recognizes that life is enriched through meaningful connections with others and the experiences we share. Through this approach, we emphasize the importance of finding joy, pursuing passions, and seeking personal fulfillment. Individuals following this approach may have a greater sense of fulfillment, happiness, and a well-rounded life. However, it is important to note that the challenges, obstacles, and hardships are inevitable. We cannot disregard or exclude the presence of struggles. The simple suggestion is that by cultivating meaningful relationships and enjoying life's experiences, individuals can better navigate and cope with the inevitable difficulties they encounter.

Now, we have to decide, "Which approach should we choose?" that ultimately depends on personal values, beliefs, and priorities. It's important to strike a balance that aligns with your own perspective. Some of you may find that the second approach works best for you, acknowledging the presence of struggle while also prioritizing relationships and personal growth.

In the first scenario, there is everything as the second one, every relationship, every feeling is there, but because of the struggle, we are not able to focus on these relationships, these feelings, these moments as most of the time we are under pressure that we are struggling.

I want to ask a question:

Is there anyone, who is not struggling?

Struggles, and challenges are inherent aspects of the human experience, and they can manifest in various forms for different individuals. Everyone faces their own unique challenges.

There are some struggles to name a few, individuals can have:

Financial Struggles:

Some individuals may face difficulties managing their finances, striving to make ends meet, or experiencing financial insecurity. On the other hand, those who have accumulated wealth may face the pressure of maintaining their financial stability and preserving their assets. The fear of losing what they have gained can create its own set of challenges and stress.

Employment Struggles:

People often encounter hurdles when searching for employment, facing competition or struggling to find a suitable job that aligns with their skills and aspirations. Conversely, individuals who are already employed may encounter challenges in their workplace, such as maintaining job satisfaction, striving for career growth, managing work-life balance, the fear of layoffs, or adapting to changing work environments.

"Let's understand it this way: Imagine a person who has been working for many years, accumulating significant experience in their field. Despite this, deep down, they harbor a fear of losing their job as they grow older. In today's fast-paced world, companies often prefer to give opportunities to younger individuals. Consequently, older employees find themselves needing to exert more effort to keep up with the younger generation.

This fear is not unfounded. The competitive job market places immense pressure on experienced professionals to continuously prove their worth. While their years of expertise are invaluable, the ever-evolving technological landscape and the fresh perspectives brought in by younger employees create a challenging environment. Older workers must work harder to stay relevant, often pushing themselves beyond their comfort zones to match the pace and adaptability of their younger counterparts."

Environmental Struggles:

Environmental factors, such as heavy rains or the absence of rainfall, can present challenges for different individuals. Excessive rainfall can lead to flooding, property damage, and transportation issues, causing struggles for those affected. Conversely, the absence of rain can lead to drought, agricultural difficulties, and water scarcity, presenting hardships for individuals and communities dependent on such resources.

Family Struggles:

Family dynamics can be a source of both support and challenge. Some individuals may face struggles within their family relationships, such as conflicts, communication issues, or balancing personal needs with familial expectations. Additionally, responsibilities and challenges associated with raising and caring for family members, especially children or elderly relatives, can also present unique struggles.

Let's understand it this way: In the quiet hours before dawn, a single mother rises, her body heavy with exhaustion but driven by the knowledge that her children depend on her. Each morning is a race against time, filled with the endless tasks of getting her children ready for school, preparing their meals, and ensuring they have everything they need for the day ahead. The home is often silent, with her children lost in their own worlds—one absorbed in the music from their headphones, the other staring blankly at the breakfast table. The mother's attempts at conversation are met with curt responses or silence, the growing distance between them becoming more apparent with each passing day.

As she heads off to work, balancing two jobs just to keep the household running, her mind frequently drifts back to her children. The once close relationship they shared seems to have frayed over time, replaced by misunderstandings and unspoken frustrations. The long hours she spends away from home, working as a waitress during the day and a cleaner in the evenings, leave little room for meaningful conversations or family time.

Her eldest child, now entering the turbulent teenage years, seems to be pulling away, retreating behind a wall of indifference. Arguments over schoolwork, curfews, and friends have become more common, with each clash leaving both sides feeling unheard and disconnected. The younger child, once full of questions and stories, has grown quieter, retreating into a world of video games, preferring their company to attempting conversations with a mother who always seems too tired or too busy.

The communication gap between mother and children has become more than just a lack of words—it's a widening chasm filled with missed connections and lost opportunities to support each other. The mother, though painfully aware of the distance growing between them, feels trapped by her responsibilities. The relentless grind of work and the overwhelming fatigue make it difficult for her to reach out, to find the right words to bridge the gap.

Even when she does come home early, the silence that greets her is heavy with unspoken emotions. The children may be present, but their attention is elsewhere—focused on screens, on anything but each other. The mother tries to engage, asking about their day or offering to help with homework, but the responses are brief and detached, leaving her feeling more isolated than ever.

She knows she is losing them, that the lack of communication is eroding the bond they once had. The pressures of being both breadwinner and sole caregiver are immense, and though she longs to connect with her children, the constant demands of survival often take precedence.

It's important to remember that in this complex situation, there are no villains. The mother's relentless drive to provide the best for her children is born out of necessity, not neglect. Her love for them is the very reason she works so hard, even though it sometimes means being apart. Meanwhile, the children's retreat into their own worlds is not a rejection of their mother but a response to the circumstances they find themselves in. They, too, are navigating a difficult reality—one where they must find their own way to cope with the absence of the attention they naturally crave.

To summarize the fact is that everyone faces struggles and challenges in their own way, regardless of their circumstances. The nature of these struggles may vary, but the common thread is that difficulties and obstacles are an inherent part of life. It reminds us that each person's journey is unique, and it encourages us to approach others with kindness, understanding, and a willingness to lend a helping hand when needed.

I believe the first approach is not that challenging, as the easiest thing for individuals is to fall into a pattern or perceive themselves as constantly struggling and to attribute all their hardships to external factors such as others or destiny. This mindset often manifests as a tendency to complain, feel victimized, and place blame on circumstances beyond their control. It can be a convenient way to shift responsibility away from oneself and seek validation or sympathy from others. This mindset can also lead to a sense of helplessness, as individuals may feel that their struggles are inevitable and beyond their ability to overcome. It can perpetuate a cycle of negativity and hinder personal growth and development.

However, the second approach is quite challenging as having all the hardships and challenges, we have to work hard to enjoy every relationship, every feeling, and every moment.

From the moment a child is born, the journey of hurdles begins. From the basic survival needs of feeding and growing, to learning how to communicate and navigate the world, each stage of life presents its own set of challenges. As we grow older, the struggles shift to different areas such as education, career, relationships, and family responsibilities. While struggles are inevitable, it is up to us to approach them with a positive mindset and find ways to enjoy life despite them. We should believe that challenges can provide us with an opportunity for growth and personal development.

Amidst the busyness of life and our focus on materialistic pursuits, it is important to remember the value of real connections and relationships. We should invest our time and effort to nurture and strengthen meaningful relationships, and believe me, this will bring immense joy and fulfillment. Genuine connections with loved ones can provide support, companionship, and a sense of belonging, enriching our lives in ways that material possessions cannot.

The uncertainty of life is a fundamental reality that we all face, and none of us knows when our time will come to an end. Therefore, it is important to live each day to the fullest, rather than simply going through the motions.

Embracing a positive outlook, approaching others with a smile, practicing forgiveness, and releasing grudges can greatly contribute to your happiness.

Holding on to negative emotions and grievances only burdens you, restraining your personal growth and hindering the ability to fully enjoy life's moments.

In our pursuits of goals and aspirations, we often find ourselves engrossed in the struggles of today, hoping that achieving those goals will bring contentment to ourselves and our families. It is not uncommon for individuals to work tirelessly, dedicating long hours to their careers or endeavors, with the belief that their efforts will secure a better future for their loved ones. This desire is fueled by the genuine desire to provide financial stability and material comforts to the family, which is absolutely acceptable.

However, it's important to recognize that amidst the pursuit of these goals, we may unintentionally neglect the precious time we have with our family and loved ones. The excuse of "doing it for family" is often used as a justification for prioritizing work or external achievements over spending quality time with our parents, children, or spouse. While the intention is well-meaning, it's crucial to consider the potential consequences of neglecting those important relationships.

I have often seen people say that they are really busy with their professional endeavors, and they will spend time with their families "some other day." However, my friend, life is really unpredictable, and we cannot guarantee that there will be a tomorrow or "some other day". Circumstances can change, and we may regret not having made the most of the time we had. It is essential to cherish and value the present moment, understanding that time is a precious gift that cannot be reclaimed once it's gone.

I want to share a story about my friend Sameer, someone who, like many of us, got caught up in the whirlwind of career ambitions. Sameer was always a driven guy, laser-focused on climbing the corporate ladder. He was known for his work ethic, and his office was always buzzing with activity. There wasn't a day where he didn't have back-to-back meetings, deadlines looming, or another business trip on the horizon. Sameer had set his sights on a big promotion, one that he believed would secure his family's future and fulfil his professional dreams.

But there was a trade-off that came with that kind of dedication. Sameer was often working late or traveling for business, which meant missing out on family dinners, bedtime stories with his daughter Simran, and quiet evenings with his wife Natasha. "I'm doing it for them," he would say, trying to ease his own guilt. "Once I get this promotion, I'll have more time for them. I'll make it up to them."

Natasha, being the understanding and supportive wife that she is, stood by him. She knew how much his work meant to him and trusted that he was doing it for their future. But over time, the strain started to show. Conversations between them grew shorter, often interrupted by Sameer's buzzing phone or the urgent need to send off a quick email. Simran, their bright and lively daughter, began to notice her father's absence. Her excitement at showing him her latest drawing or telling him about her day slowly faded as she realized he was too busy to listen.

Sameer didn't see the changes at first. He was so caught up in his work, so focused on the prize at the end of the tunnel, that he didn't notice the growing distance between him and Natasha or the way Simran's laughter seemed quieter when he was around. To him, everything was fine—he was working hard, providing for his family, and believing that soon, they would all enjoy the benefits.

Then one Friday afternoon, everything changed. Sameer was in the middle of an important meeting when Natasha called. He was annoyed at the interruption and sent it to voicemail. But Natasha kept calling, and each time, it felt more urgent. Finally, frustrated, he stepped out to answer.

"Sameer," Natasha's voice was trembling, a sound he'd never heard before. "It's Simran...she's in the hospital. There was an accident..."

Time seemed to stop for Sameer. He could barely process the words as Natasha explained what had happened. Simran had been playing in the yard when she fell and hit her head. She was unconscious, and the doctors were running tests. The word "serious" echoed in his ears, drowning out everything else.

Sameer raced to the hospital, his heart pounding in his chest. The drive felt endless, each second stretching into eternity. When he finally arrived, he found Natasha in the waiting room, her face pale and tear-streaked. She collapsed into his arms, sobbing uncontrollably.

"I'm so sorry," Sameer whispered, his voice breaking. "I should have been there..."

The next few hours were a blur—doctors, medical terms that he barely understood, and the sterile smell of the hospital. Sameer sat by Simran's bedside, holding her small hand in his, willing her to wake up. As he looked at his daughter, lying there so still and fragile, the weight of his choices came crashing down on him.

All those late nights, the missed moments, the promises of "tomorrow"—they suddenly felt so empty, so meaningless. He had been chasing success, believing he was doing it for his family, but in doing so, he had neglected the very people he loved most. The time he thought he could reclaim later was now gone, replaced by a terrifying uncertainty.

When Simran finally opened her eyes, Sameer felt a wave of relief so intense it brought him to tears. She was groggy, confused, but alive. The doctors assured them she would recover, but it would take time.

As they brought Simran home, Sameer vowed never to take his family for granted again. The promotion, the accolades, the financial security—none of it mattered as much as the simple joy of being with loved ones. He realized that the true measure of success wasn't in titles or paychecks, but in the time spent with those you love.

Sameer began to make changes. He started leaving work at a reasonable hour, turning down extra projects, and making sure he was present for every family dinner, every school event, and every quiet evening at home. It wasn't easy—there were still demands from his job—but he had learned a hard lesson: time is a precious gift, one that cannot be reclaimed once it's gone.

He started to rebuild his relationship with Natasha and Simran, not through grand gestures, but through consistent, everyday moments. Slowly, the laughter returned to their home, the warmth and connection that had been missing for so long. Sameer knew he couldn't change the past, but he could cherish the present and make the most of the time they had together.

Sameer's story is a reminder that while our intentions may be well-meaning, it's easy to lose sight of what truly matters. The pursuit of success and the desire to provide for our loved ones can sometimes blind us to the importance of being there for them. Life is unpredictable, and "some other day" might never come. It's up to us to cherish the moments we have now and to recognize that the greatest gift we can give our loved ones is our time and attention.

The whole point is, while it is vital to work hard and strive for the betterment of our families, we should recognize that the most valuable gift we can offer is our time and presence. Material possessions may provide temporary comfort, but the emotional connection and love that come from spending quality moments together are priceless.

Finding a balance between work commitments and spending time with loved ones is key. It requires setting priorities, managing time effectively, and being intentional about creating opportunities for meaningful interactions. Making an effort to be present, actively engage, and foster genuine connections can create lasting memories that cannot be replaced by material possessions alone.

It is not uncommon to hear people express their success in work, in financial stability, and the support they receive from their family and friends. While it is heartening to have the backing of their loved ones, it is important to consider whether they are genuinely happy or fulfilled.

Often, family members are inclined to support and celebrate the achievements of their loved ones. They may express joy and pride, even if they themselves are facing personal challenges and sacrificing their own happiness for the sake of the family unit. This can create a perception that everyone is content when, in reality, individual happiness may vary.

Taking the time to understand the true well-being and happiness of family members requires sincere effort and open communication. It involves going beyond surface-level interactions and actively listening to their thoughts, concerns, and desires.

We often find ourselves saying, "I just don't have time because of work." But let's be honest—this is just an excuse. We can always make time for what truly matters to us. The key is to weave these important moments into our daily routine.

Think about it: many of us create a daily schedule, planning out what to do and when. It's a great habit because it helps our day run smoothly. But have you ever wondered why we do this? We plan so that everything flows efficiently, and when things are pre-planned, the results are always better.

Now, let's use this strategy to prioritize what's most important. Imagine starting your day with breakfast alongside your family and kids. No phones, just meaningful conversations. It sounds simple, but trust me, incorporating this one habit into your routine can bring about a significant positive change in your life.

And why stop there? You can create other small but impactful habits. For example, make it a point to call your family at least once during your workday. Surely, you can spare two minutes for a quick check-in. This tiny effort can mean a lot and make your loved ones feel valued and connected.

By consciously carving out time for what really matters, we're not just scheduling tasks—we're enriching our lives. So, let's stop making excuses and start making moments that count.

How can we ensure that our family and loved ones are really happy?

As individuals, it is our responsibility to ensure the happiness of our loved ones. This can be achieved by prioritizing quality time spent together and actively participating in their lives. Instead of deferring these moments for the future, it is crucial to seize the present and create meaningful memories.

"By spending TODAY with our family and loved ones, not TOMORROW"

As humans, it is a common tendency to compare our own lives to those of others and perceive that "the grass is always greener on the other side." This saying reflects the practice to believe that others have a better or a more desirable life while disregarding the values and blessings present in our lives.

The other reason for this perception is that we often focus on what we lack or desire, rather than appreciating what we already have. This mindset leads to a constant longing for what others possess, whether it's material possessions, achievements, or perceived success.

Why it happens, because instead of watering the grass on our side, we become preoccupied with the illusion that the grass is greener elsewhere. This mindset prevents us from fully embracing and enjoying the present moment and can lead to a perpetual state of dissatisfaction and struggle.

What we can do to counter this pattern:

We can shift our focus and cultivate gratitude for the blessings in our lives. Taking time to acknowledge and appreciate what we have allows us to recognize the beauty and value of our own grass.

It is also important to understand that appearances can be deceiving. While it may seem like others have it all together, they too have their own struggles and challenges. No one's life is perfect, and everyone faces their own set of difficulties.

Therefore, it is essential to redirect our attention to our lives and practice gratitude, so that we can develop a healthier perspective. Rather than constantly striving for what others have, we should allow us to appreciate our unique journey, focus on personal growth, and find joy in the present moment.

Rather than viewing life as a constant struggle, it is always beneficial to approach it as a beautiful journey. Embracing the ups and downs, the joys and challenges, and the opportunities for growth and self-discovery, we can transform our perspective and find meaning in every experience. Life is meant to be lived, savored, and appreciated.

Expressing gratitude to a higher power, the universe, or a source of inspiration one believes in, such as thanking God, can provide a sense of humility, perspective, and spiritual connection. Recognizing life as a beautiful gift from the Almighty allows us to approach each day with a positive mindset and an open heart.

Chapter 8

Patience is the key

A few days ago, I visited Rishikesh. It was evening, and I was sitting by the banks of the Ganges River. Not far from me, a gentleman sat hunched over, his shoulders drooping as if the weight of the world rested upon them. His hands were clasped tightly, knuckles white, as he stared vacantly at the water, the gentle flow of the river seemingly lost on him. Concerned, I approached him and asked, "Brother, are you okay? If you have any problems, you can share them with me."

It seemed as though he had been waiting for someone to break the silence that had engulfed him. His eyes, red-rimmed and weary, met mine, and for a moment, they flickered with a glimmer of hope before dimming again. With a heavy sigh, he began to speak, his voice low and tinged with bitterness.

"Nothing good is happening in my life," he said, his voice cracking under the strain of unspoken grief.

"I don't know what to do. It feels like I am being punished for the sins I must have committed." He paused, his hands trembling slightly as he ran them through his disheveled hair. "I engage in a lot of worship, charity, and come here every year to take a dip in the Ganges, as they say that taking a dip in the Ganges washes away all sins. But that's not happening with me."

He looked down at his hands, as if searching for answers in the lines etched into his skin. "Once," he continued, his voice barely above a whisper, "I believed that every prayer I offered, every act of charity was heard and answered. I remember the first time I took a dip in the Ganges. I was filled with a sense of peace, convinced that all my burdens had been washed away. But now... now, I feel nothing. It's like the water doesn't reach my soul anymore."

As he spoke, his eyes filled with unshed tears, and the muscles in his face tightened, reflecting the inner turmoil that words alone could not convey. His despair was palpable, a deep-rooted pain that seemed to have taken hold of him, refusing to let go.

I listened to his words, feeling the depth of his disillusionment. I tried to comfort him, saying, "Don't worry, everything will be fine." But even as the words left my lips, I could sense that they offered little solace. After a while, he left, his footsteps heavy as he walked away, leaving me to sit alone, watching the Ganges. His words echoed in my mind, not just in their content but in the way they had been spoken—with a profound sense of loss that went beyond faith. His despair made me reflect deeply.

The setting sun cast a golden hue over the flowing river, and I couldn't help but ponder the gentleman's plight. It made me question the common beliefs we hold about religious rituals and their impact on our lives. Are these practices merely symbolic, or do they hold a deeper significance that we often fail to understand?

As the cool breeze from the river brushed against my face, I realized that perhaps the true essence of these rituals lies not just in the act itself but in the sincerity and intention behind them. The gentleman's struggle was not just with his circumstances but with his faith, which seemed to be waning despite his efforts to hold on to it.

In that serene moment by the Ganges, it became clear to me that faith is not just about rituals. It's about the strength we derive from them and the hope they instill in us to keep moving forward despite the challenges. The man's frustration was a reflection of a common human experience - the search for meaning and solace in times of distress.

This encounter left me contemplating the nature of faith and the ways we seek comfort in our traditions. It underscored the importance of inner belief and the peace that comes from within, rather than just the external acts of devotion.

When a person faces difficulties in life, such thoughts often arise in their mind, but in reality, it isn't so. I believe that no matter how many sins a person has committed, if they sincerely and wholeheartedly worship God and take a dip in the Ganges, their sins can indeed be washed away, provided they do not repeat those sinful actions. However, humans often fail to uphold this, and instead, they blame the rituals, saying that these are just sayings and that they've tried everything to no avail.

This common sentiment arises when people don't see immediate results from their efforts. They become disillusioned, feeling that their sincere actions and devotions are in vain. The key lies in the continuation and consistency of one's efforts and faith. Rituals like bathing in the Ganges are not just about the physical act but also about the internal transformation they inspire. The real challenge is to maintain purity of heart and intention after performing these rituals.

Often, people expect an instant change, a miraculous turnaround in their fortunes, without considering the importance of sustained inner change. The act of taking a dip in the holy river symbolizes a new beginning, a commitment to a better path. It requires not just the cleansing of the body but also a deep commitment to cleanse one's soul and actions.

The failure to see change is not due to the inefficacy of the rituals themselves but rather the lack of sustained personal change and commitment to righteousness. Blaming the rituals is easier than acknowledging the difficulty of true inner transformation. The real test of faith and devotion lies in continuously striving to be better, even when immediate results are not visible.

It is a well-known adage that to err is human. When God crafted mankind, He was well aware that humans would make mistakes. After all, if humans were incapable of error, wouldn't they be gods themselves? The only truly infallible being is God. Mistakes are an intrinsic part of human nature; sometimes they are made knowingly, while other times they occur unwittingly. Regardless of the intent, mistakes are inevitable, and with them come consequences.

This is why it is often recommended that one should engage in acts of charity and perform virtuous deeds to counterbalance the repercussions of their errors.

Consider the analogy of someone who has gained a significant amount of weight. To control their weight, they avoid unhealthy, fried, and harmful foods and instead focus on consuming nutritious meals. They begin to exercise and run to maintain their health. In much the same way, engaging in prayers, performing acts of charity, and doing good deeds can help counteract the negative effects of one's wrongdoings.

Engaging in these positive actions isn't merely about erasing sins or avoiding punishment; it is about striving for a better self, for a life aligned with moral and spiritual values. Just as one would take deliberate steps to improve physical health, one must also take conscious steps to nurture their spiritual well-being.

Moreover, when a person acknowledges their mistakes and makes an effort to atone through good deeds, it demonstrates personal growth and a sincere desire to lead a righteous life. It’s not just about counteracting negative actions with positive ones but about fundamentally transforming one's behavior and mindset.

Charity and good deeds act as a spiritual exercise regimen, essential for maintaining the health of the soul. They help in creating a balance, fostering inner peace, and paving the way for a more meaningful and harmonious life. Thus, just as physical fitness requires ongoing effort and discipline, so does spiritual fitness.

Specific acts of charity, such as providing food and clothing to the homeless, sponsoring a child's education, or volunteering time at a local community center, serve as tangible ways to give back and contribute to the well-being of others. Similarly, donating to causes that uplift underprivileged communities, planting trees to improve the environment, or simply helping a neighbor in need can have profound impacts—not only on those receiving the help but also on the person giving it." But it's not looking very promising.

It is important to note that these actions do not entirely erase one's sins. However, they do provide the strength and resilience needed to withstand the adverse outcomes associated with those sins. Through sincere efforts in doing good, individuals can find the fortitude to face the challenges posed by their past mistakes.

However, human nature is such that we often seek immediate results. We want instant gratification. When someone prays in the morning, they expect a miracle by evening. If they donate to charity today, they believe they will receive even greater rewards tomorrow. But when things don't unfold this way, their faith begins to waver. For a while, they persist, but eventually, they conclude that there is no point if nothing seems to be changing.

This is where they make a grave mistake, one that surpasses all other mistakes made in life. Unlike other errors that might be unintentional, this one is committed knowingly. At the very moment when patience and faith are most needed, the individual gives up.

It's essential to understand that miracles in life don't happen overnight. Every good deed, every act of worship, charity, and righteousness yields its fruits gradually. It's a continuous process that demands time and patience. Just as a seed takes time to grow into a tree, our good actions also take time to manifest their rewards.

This doesn't mean that efforts are in vain. On the contrary, it signifies that we must maintain our belief and patience in our actions. Small, consistent efforts every day eventually lead to significant outcomes.

At some point in life, everyone comes to the realization of the mistakes they have made and the wrongs they have committed. The difference lies only in how soon one recognizes this—some realize it early, while others take much longer. Once this awareness sets in, a person often seeks ways to rectify these mistakes. They consult priests, wise individuals, and take their advice, engaging in rituals, charity, and other remedial actions. Visits to temples become frequent, and they pray fervently to the divine for forgiveness and guidance.

However, it is crucial to understand that when a person embarks on this path of seeking forgiveness and making amends, they are inherently acknowledging their wrongdoings. They accept that they have committed sins and are willing to make efforts to atone for them. They start with great enthusiasm—performing rituals, donating, and following various prescribed remedies diligently for days, weeks, or even months.

Yet, often, as time passes, and they don't see immediate or significant results, their fervor begins to wane. The efforts they initially put into these practices gradually diminish. Disheartened by the lack of visible change or improvement, they start to abandon the very practices they believed would bring them redemption and peace. This cycle of initial enthusiasm followed by disillusionment is a common human experience, reflecting the challenge of maintaining faith and persistence in the face of delayed gratification.

Everyone desires the blessings and grace of God, but the patience and faith required to attain that grace are often lacking. Imagine a person who suddenly feels the weight of their misdeeds at the age of 30, 35, or 40. They decide to turn over a new leaf, engaging in good deeds and seeking divine forgiveness. However, they must realize that it took decades to accumulate those wrongdoings, and it will take considerable time and consistent effort to counterbalance them with virtuous actions.

God grants whatever is asked for with a sincere heart, showing no discrimination. Our scriptures and ancient texts also describe how anyone who has earnestly worshiped God—whether a saint or a demon—has been granted divine boons.

An illustrative example of this is Ravana, the king of Lanka from the Hindu epic, the Ramayana.

Ravana was a powerful demon king who, despite his eventual antagonistic role, was known for his intense devotion and dedication. His story is a testament to the idea that divine grace is not about who we are by birth or status but about the purity and persistence of our actions and intentions.

Ravana performed rigorous penance and worshipped Lord Shiva with unwavering focus and devotion. His dedication was so profound that he is said to have offered his own heads—one by one—as sacrifices to appease the deity. Shiva, moved by Ravana's sincerity and determination, granted him a boon, making him invincible and endowed with immense power.

Yet, Ravana's story also underscores a crucial lesson: divine grace requires not just devotion but the right application of that grace. Despite his immense power and devotion, Ravana's flaws, including his arrogance and desire for control, ultimately led to his downfall. His story reflects that while patience and focus are vital, they must be aligned with righteous conduct and wisdom.

This example emphasizes that the divine grants blessings based on the purity and persistence of one's actions and intentions, rather than one's status or identity. It reminds us that true spiritual growth and divine favor come from a balanced combination of sincere devotion and ethical behavior.

True devotion and the pursuit of divine grace are not about quick fixes but about a sustained, heartfelt journey.

But those were different times. Today, we live in an era where it's said that the greatest act of virtue is helping those in need. However, it's important to remember that true help should be offered quietly, without seeking recognition. When we help someone, it should be done in such a way that one hand doesn't know what the other is doing. These days, it's common to see people posting videos on social media, showcasing their acts of charity towards the less fortunate. These videos often receive a flood of praise and admiration, but I believe this isn't true charity. Real virtue lies in selfless acts, done with a pure heart and without any hidden motives. Unfortunately, the motive behind many of these videos is often self-promotion—gaining fame or attracting more views on social media.

In reality, they are helping themselves more than they are helping the poor. We all ask for something in life, but poverty is a curse that strips away dignity. Imagine the mental state of a person who has to beg on the streets, sacrificing their self-respect for survival. It's a profound and painful experience that's hard for most of us to truly understand. Yet, some people film these moments, add emotional music, and post them online. To me, this isn't helping the poor—it's exploiting their misery.

In our digital age, where everyone is eager to display their good deeds, we risk losing the essence of genuine kindness. True help is offered without an audience, without the need for applause. The sincerity of our actions is measured by our willingness to remain unseen, to help without expecting anything in return.

Imagine a world where help is given purely out of compassion. Helping the poor means respecting their dignity and addressing their needs, not turning their struggles into a spectacle for personal gain. We must remember that every act of kindness should be rooted in empathy and respect.

Our scriptures are replete with examples of individuals who have pleased the gods through intense penance and have been granted boons. However, many times, those whose intentions were impure or who misused their acquired powers faced dire consequences themselves.

The sins we commit knowingly are within our awareness, but those committed unknowingly are countless and beyond our reckoning. We may not always remember the misdeeds that have accumulated over time. However, we have control over the good deeds we perform. Keeping track of our good actions is within our grasp, and as for how long we should continue performing them, there is no definitive limit.

Faith and patience are the pillars of a virtuous life. Just as countless sages and devotees in our scriptures maintained their devotion despite adversities, we too should strive to keep our faith steadfast. This faith is not just in the divine but also in the process of doing good.

Life is an ongoing journey of self-improvement and growth. The good deeds we do today might not show immediate results, but they gradually build a reservoir of positive karma. This karma eventually manifests in ways we might not even anticipate, often balancing out the negative influences of our past actions.

Think of it as planting seeds. We may not see the fruits immediately, but with consistent care and nurturing, these seeds grow into strong trees bearing abundant fruit. Similarly, our good deeds, performed with sincerity and patience, will eventually lead to a life filled with peace and blessings.

So, keep faith in God, remain patient, and commit to performing as many good deeds as possible. Over time, you'll notice the positive impact on your life, bringing balance and harmony to your existence.

Let's strive to make our good deeds invisible to the world, but deeply felt by those we help.

Chapter 9

Are You a Good Listener?

As human beings, we naturally desire to be heard and understood when we express ourselves to others. We long for genuine connection and empathy from those we interact with. However, in our quest to be heard, do we extend the same courtesy to others? Do we truly listen, or do we merely wait for our turn to speak?

Being a good listener entails more than just hearing the words someone else is saying. It involves actively engaging with them, empathizing with their perspective, and seeking to understand their feelings and motivations. It requires setting aside our own preconceived notions and biases to fully immerse ourselves in their world.

Think about the last time you had a conversation with someone. Were you truly present in that moment, or were you mentally elsewhere, formulating your response before they had finished speaking? Being present and attentive in conversations is crucial for fostering meaningful connections and building trust with others.

Moreover, being a good listener goes beyond the spoken word. It involves paying attention to nonverbal cues such as body language, tone of voice, and facial expressions. These subtle signals often convey more than words alone and provide valuable insight into the speaker's emotions and underlying thoughts.

Let's dive into a scenario that might resonate with many of us. Imagine a husband coming home after a long, grueling day at work. He's been reprimanded by his boss, had to scold some of his team members, and even got into a heated argument with another driver on his way back. On the other side of the day, his wife has had her own share of troubles. She's been tackling household chores since morning, especially since their maid took an unexpected leave. This meant she had to do all the cleaning and cooking herself. When she went to the kitchen to prepare lunch, she discovered they were out of gas. Thinking quickly, she decided to pick up some food on her way to get the kids from school. At the market, she ordered takeout from a restaurant, but faced another hurdle when her online payment wouldn't go through due to network issues. Luckily, the shopkeeper knew her and allowed her to pay later. She brought the kids home, set the table, and just as they were about to eat, the power went out.

Now, let's picture her mental state. By evening, when her husband arrives, they sit down for a cup of tea. She's about to unload her day's burdens when her husband jumps in first, venting about his terrible day. Overwhelmed by her own challenges, she finds it nearly impossible to focus on his grievances. It's not her fault; after a day like hers, who could blame her for not being able to fully engage? Consequently, she ends up bottling up her own struggles because her husband is already visibly stressed.

Here's where a little empathy could make a world of difference. If the husband were to notice his wife's weary expression and ask, "Is something wrong? You seem upset," she might feel understood and open up about her day. This mutual sharing could lead to a meaningful conversation and maybe even some solutions to their problems. But if they both remain wrapped up in their own frustrations, the husband might feel that his wife is indifferent to his problems, and she might feel the same. This could create unnecessary tension and distance between them.

This scenario teaches us an important lesson: when we come home, we should spend a few moments truly paying attention to each other, trying to understand the unspoken struggles our loved ones might be facing. This principle isn't limited to just-married couples. It applies to all relationships—at work with colleagues, with our bosses, and with our friends. We should always strive to be more empathetic and attentive to the people around us, fostering understanding, and connection in every interaction.

Unfortunately, in today's fast-paced world filled with distractions and constant stimulation, genuine listening has become a rare commodity. We are often too busy checking our phones, scrolling through social media, or thinking about our own concerns to truly listen to those around us.

But the art of listening is not lost; it simply requires conscious effort and practice. By cultivating mindfulness and being fully present in our interactions, we can become better listeners and, in turn, cultivate deeper connections with others.

In the cacophony of life's demands and distractions, the art of listening often remains overlooked, overshadowed by the clamor of our own thoughts and concerns. Yet, it is in the quietude of attentive listening that the symphony of human connection finds its melody. It is a skill that, once mastered, has the power to dissolve barriers, foster empathy, and nurture profound relationships.

While the ability to assert oneself is undeniably important, the true essence of effective communication lies in the art of listening. Without earnestly attending to another person's words, we risk missing out on the nuances of their perspective, thus hindering the potential for genuine understanding and empathy. By prioritizing active listening, we transcend the surface of conversation, delving into the depths of shared human experience and fostering profound connections.

However, the path to becoming a skilled listener is not without its challenges. It requires the cultivation of two essential virtues: time and self-discipline. By valuing the precious currency of time and exercising disciplined restraint, individuals empower themselves to engage fully in the act of listening. This deliberate investment not only enriches their own lives but also amplifies their capacity to positively influence and uplift those around them. This creates a ripple effect of empathy and understanding in the world.

In the hustle and bustle of modern life, with its myriad challenges and complexities, it's rare to find someone who isn't grappling with their own set of worries and concerns. From the pressures of work and family to the constant barrage of information and stimuli, navigating the intricacies of daily existence can feel like a never-ending battle. Yet, amidst the chaos, there lies a profound truth: the power of listening and understanding.

When faced with adversity, we often seek solace and guidance from those closest to us or professional counselors. We turn to them in search of solutions, hoping for clarity and resolution in the face of uncertainty. However, the key to unlocking these solutions lies not only in seeking advice but also in truly understanding the nature of the problem at hand.

Indeed, there's an age-old adage that suggests every problem has a solution, provided we first understand the problem itself. But therein lies the challenge: who among us truly understands? In a world consumed by the demands of everyday life, where everyone is preoccupied with their own struggles and challenges, genuine understanding can feel like a rare commodity.

However, the importance of listening and understanding extends far beyond the realm of problem-solving alone; it permeates every facet of our lives. Consider, for instance, the classroom setting, where the diligent student who listens attentively to the teacher's words invariably reaps the rewards of academic success. Conversely, those who allow their attention to wander are left to contend with the consequences of their inattention.

Similarly, in the realm of personal relationships, when a friend or loved one confides in us with their innermost concerns, they bestow upon us a sacred trust. It is incumbent upon us, therefore, to honor that trust with the utmost sincerity and compassion. We must afford them the gift of our undivided attention, granting them the time and space to articulate their thoughts and feelings without reservation or judgment

The act of listening is an affirmation of our shared humanity, a testament to our capacity for empathy and understanding. It is through the attentive ear and compassionate heart that we forge bonds of trust and companionship, navigating life's myriad challenges with grace and resilience.

As I've previously mentioned, the ability to listen attentively resides within each of us, yet it often remains underutilized. Nevertheless, like any skill, it can be honed and refined through diligent practice and conscious effort.

In my view, cultivating the art of listening begins with a mindful approach to our interactions with others. When engaged in conversation, it's imperative to direct our full attention towards the speaker, setting aside distractions and internal chatter. By doing so, we create a space where the speaker feels valued and respected, fostering an environment conducive to open and honest communication.

Moreover, effective listening entails more than just hearing the words spoken; it involves attuning ourselves to the speaker's nonverbal cues and subtleties. Body language, facial expressions, and tone of voice can often convey more than words alone, providing valuable insight into the speaker's emotions and underlying sentiments. Thus, it's essential to remain attuned to these signals, allowing them to guide our understanding of the speaker's perspective.

In instances where verbal communication may falter or fall short, such as when a speaker hesitates to express themselves fully, it becomes paramount to rely on our ability to interpret nonverbal cues. By observing facial expressions, gestures, and posture, we can glean additional context and meaning, enriching our comprehension of the speaker's message.

Furthermore, it's crucial to approach moments of uncertainty or confusion with humility and openness. If ever in doubt or struggling to grasp the speaker's intent, do not hesitate to seek clarification. Asking questions such as "Am I understanding correctly?" or "Could you please elaborate on that point?" demonstrates a genuine commitment to understanding and validates the speaker's perspective.

However, it's important to exercise restraint and refrain from interjecting with our own thoughts or opinions prematurely. Instead, allow the speaker to express themselves fully before offering any insights or reflections of your own. By doing so, we demonstrate respect for the speaker's autonomy and create a supportive space for authentic dialogue to flourish.

Truly understanding someone else's perspective requires more than just passive listening; it demands a willingness to immerse ourselves fully in their world. Instead of hastily forming judgments or opinions, we should take the time to delve deeper into the matter, gathering additional information and insights along the way.

Imagine encountering a song for the first time, one that fails to resonate with you initially. However, as you navigate through life's experiences and challenges, you find yourself revisiting that same song, only to discover a newfound appreciation and connection. Suddenly, its lyrics and melodies seem to mirror your own journey, offering solace and insight in unexpected ways.

This phenomenon underscores the importance of context and perspective in shaping our understanding and interpretation of any given situation. Just as our appreciation for a song may evolve over time, so too can our comprehension of someone else's viewpoint deepen with continued reflection and introspection.

Similarly, when seeking to comprehend another person's viewpoint, we must strive to adopt a similar level of immersion and empathy. By stepping into their shoes and viewing the situation from their perspective, we can gain a deeper appreciation for their thoughts and feelings. This requires setting aside our preconceived notions and biases, allowing ourselves to be fully present and engaged in the conversation.

Furthermore, immersing ourselves in the environment is crucial for fostering genuine empathy and understanding. Just as we connect with a song on a personal level when it mirrors our own experiences, immersing ourselves in someone else's narrative enables us to grasp the intricacies of their perspective more fully.

Before we vocalize our thoughts and opinions, it's not uncommon to experience a barrage of apprehensions and doubts. We may find ourselves questioning how our words will be perceived by others, fearing potential judgment or misunderstanding. Such concerns often stem from a desire to be accepted and understood, as well as a fear of rejection or ridicule.

Similarly, we may hesitate to share our perspectives out of fear of causing offense or discomfort to those around us. We worry that our opinions may be met with resistance or disagreement, leading to strained relationships or awkward interactions. These anxieties can be particularly pronounced when discussing sensitive or controversial topics, where the stakes feel higher and emotions run deeper.

However, amidst these doubts and insecurities, it's essential to remember the value of authenticity and sincerity in our interactions. True friendship and genuine care for others entail a commitment to honesty and integrity, even when it may be uncomfortable or challenging to do so. Instead of prioritizing temporary appeasement or avoiding conflict at all costs, we should strive to offer opinions that are grounded in empathy, respect, and genuine concern for the well-being of others.

Ultimately, the goal should not be to please or placate others but to engage in meaningful and constructive dialogue that promotes mutual understanding and growth.

Imagine being in a bustling club, where the music pounds relentlessly, drowning out all other sounds. In such an environment, trying to have a meaningful conversation becomes a daunting task. The cacophony of noise disrupts our thoughts, making it challenging to focus and comprehend the words spoken by those around us. Our minds struggle to find stillness amidst the chaos, hindering our ability to truly listen and connect with others.

In much the same way, our inner world can be filled with its own noise—the incessant chatter of thoughts, worries, and emotions that clamor for attention. It's the chatter of our minds, the echoes of past experiences, and the worries about the future—all clamoring for dominance in our consciousness. These internal distractions create a barrier between ourselves and the outside world, impeding our capacity to understand and empathize with others. Just as the external noise in the club drowns out conversation, the internal noise within us muddles our perception and distorts our understanding of the world. We may nod along to the conversation, but our thoughts are elsewhere, lost in the maze of our own concerns and distractions.

But what if we could quiet the noise within? What if we could find moments of stillness amidst the chaos of our minds? By learning to silence the inner turmoil, we open ourselves up to a deeper understanding of life and human connection. In the silence, we find clarity. In the stillness, we discover insight. And in the absence of noise, we uncover the true essence of our existence. As the mental chatter subsides, our senses become heightened, and our awareness expands. Suddenly, the world around us comes into sharper focus, and we find ourselves truly present in the moment.

We become attuned to the subtle nuances of communication—the inflections in someone's voice, the expressions flickering across their face, silencing your phone during conversations, and observingthe unspoken emotions hiding beneath the surface. Our listening becomes more than just hearing; it becomes a form of active engagement, a genuine effort to connect with others on a deeper level.

In this state of inner stillness, life takes on a new clarity and meaning. We find ourselves better equipped to navigate the complexities of human interaction, to forge deeper connections with those around us, and to gain profound insights into ourselves and the world we inhabit.

Quiet your internal noise, and you will discover a world of understanding waiting to be explored—a world where the symphony of life can be heard and appreciated in all its richness and complexity.

To truly understand life, we must first learn to listen.

Chapter 10

Beyond First Impression

I believe that our mind is a remarkable and intricate creation that possesses immense power. It serves as a gateway to our thoughts, emotions, and actions. Within the intricate realms of our minds, the images we construct of people or situations play a pivotal role, as they have the capacity to influence our perceptions and endure for significant periods. Images of something or someone that we make in our mind, have a profound impact. They act as the lenses through which we view the world, coloring our interactions, decisions, and overall outlook on life.

We live in a world where judgments are often formed in an instant. There is an old saying that echoes through the ages: "First impression is the last impression." However, according to my own experiences and reflections, I have come to believe that while first impressions hold weight, they should not be regarded as the final verdict on someone's character or potential. The perception we create of individuals can determine our level of trust, admiration, or skepticism towards them. Similarly, the impressions we form of various situations can shape our expectations, responses, and subsequent experiences. They can shape our beliefs and attitudes, subtly or profoundly influencing our interactions and relationships. Positive images can foster empathy, connection, and growth, while negative ones may breed skepticism, distance, and missed opportunities.

Impressions, I have come to understand, are intricately tied to the circumstances in which they occur. They are influenced by a myriad of factors, such as the situation at hand, the mood of an individual, their personalities, the people around them, and even the place where the incident takes place. However, two primary factors often play a significant role in shaping our initial impressions: the situation and the mood.

To elaborate on it more, let's imagine you are starting your first day of college. As you step into the classroom, the atmosphere feels tense. The teacher, standing at the front, is pacing back and forth with quick, agitated steps. His face is stern, eyes narrowed as if searching for something amiss. Without warning, he slams a book onto the desk, the sound echoing through the room, causing several students to jump in their seats.

His voice is sharp, cutting through the silence like a blade. "Why are you all so disorganized?" he snaps, glaring at the students who are still settling into their seats. The tone of his voice is harsh, devoid of warmth or patience, as if each word is a reprimand.

When a student hesitantly raises a hand to ask a question, the teacher's response is curt, almost dismissive. "Didn't you read the syllabus? This is basic knowledge!" His words are laced with irritation, and he doesn't bother to hide his frustration. There's no room for mistakes in his classroom, and it becomes painfully clear that he expects nothing less than perfection.

Naturally, you might develop a negative impression of this teacher, and you will carry this impression of him throughout the session. And now that you have made an image in your mind, you will not be able to see the good in him. But can this first impression truly be the last?

In my opinion, the answer is no. Consider that perhaps the teacher had a terrible morning, filled with personal conflicts, financial stress, or family arguments. On that particular day, several reasons could have contributed to their behavior. As time passes, you might come to realize that this seemingly strict teacher is, in fact, one of the best educators and individuals you have encountered.

Similar situations can arise when meeting new people. Sometimes, we may not find someone initially appealing or compatible with our tastes and preferences. Yet, after spending some more time with them, we may discover that they possess qualities that make them one of our closest friends.

The same principle applies in professional settings. In an office environment, you may encounter colleagues or superiors who leave a negative first impression. However, as you work alongside them and observe their dedication, skills, and unique perspectives, you might find yourself appreciating their value and forming strong professional relationships.

Consider the scenario of interviewing a job candidate. Let's say an individual enters the interview room wearing wrinkled clothes with stains on their shirt. In that moment, you might immediately form an image of their personality and decide not to hire them. However, if you proceed with the interview and give them a fair chance, you may discover that their academic qualifications, communication skills, and confidence exceed your expectations. They might even become one of your most exceptional hires, proving that first impressions can be deceiving.

Love, too, is not immune to the influence of first impressions. Personal experience has shown me that even when a first encounter with a potential partner might not leave a positive impression, it does not necessarily mean that a deep and lasting connection cannot be forged. In fact, my own wife once confessed that her initial impression of me was far from favorable. Yet, we have been together for almost 20 years and happily married, demonstrating that love can transcend first impression and grow through understanding, compassion, and shared experiences.

It is essential to note that I am not advocating for disregarding first impressions altogether. They undeniably have an impact and can create lasting effects. However, it is crucial not to let them become the sole basis of our judgments. Instead, we should approach initial judgments with caution, acknowledging that they are not the complete picture.

The motivation behind sharing my opinion on first Impressions stems from my belief that we should strive to avoid quick judgments and give people more opportunities to showcase their true selves. I believe in affording individuals multiple chances to prove themselves. Life is filled with critics, but it is through appreciation and understanding that we can foster growth and create a more compassionate society. Before rushing to judgment, let us remember that people are multi-dimensional, and their true worth may only be revealed when given the opportunity to shine.

So, let's not be hasty in our assessments. Let us give people the benefit of doubt and provide them with the space to reveal their hidden potential. By doing so, we can unlock the extraordinary qualities that lie beneath the surface, enriching our own lives and fostering a world that thrives on empathy and understanding.

Chapter 11

One More Life

Life is a puzzle wrapped in a mystery, isn't it? People often find themselves grappling with the complexities of existence, wondering what it truly entails. The age-old question persists: What is life, really? Is it a canvas we paint with our dreams and aspirations, or is it a script already penned by the hand of fate? It's a conundrum that has puzzled minds for centuries.

Consider this: if life were merely the manifestation of our childhood fantasies, then discontent and despair would be alien concepts. As a child, one's imagination runs wild with visions of the future, filled with happiness and success. We dream of a life where every wish is fulfilled, every goal achieved. But as we journey through life, we realize that reality often diverges from our dreams. We encounter obstacles, face setbacks, and question whether our destinies are truly in our hands.

If life is indeed predestined, then does it mean that every twist and turn, every joy and sorrow, is predetermined? Are we merely actors following a script written long before we took our first breath? These are the questions that haunt the human psyche, seeking answers in the enigmatic tapestry of existence.

Once again, we stand at the crossroads of existential inquiry, grappling with the enigmatic concept of life's true essence. It unfolds before us like a multifaceted gem, its brilliance radiating from the juxtaposition of our aspirations against the backdrop of destiny's grand design.

The tension between free will and destiny is a theme that has transcended cultures and eras, finding expression in the wisdom of both Western and Eastern philosophies. In the Bhagavad Gita, an ancient Indian text, this tension is brought to life through a profound dialogue between Prince Arjuna and the God Krishna. Arjuna, standing on the battlefield of Kurukshetra, is paralyzed by doubt and moral dilemma. He is torn between his duty as a warrior and the devastation that fulfilling this duty will bring upon his own kin.

Krishna, in his divine wisdom, counsels Arjuna on the nature of duty (dharma) and the broader cosmic order. He reveals that while each person has a role to play in the grand scheme of life, this role must be performed with detachment from the outcomes. Krishna advises Arjuna to act according to his dharma, to fulfill his responsibilities with unwavering resolve, but without attachment to success or failure. This teaching encapsulates a nuanced balance between free will and the inevitability of fate.

Krishna's counsel suggests that while the circumstances we face may be shaped by forces beyond our control, how we respond to these circumstances remains within our power. The essence of free will lies in this response–in the choices we make, the actions we take, and the attitude with which we approach our duties. Yet, Krishna also acknowledges the presence of a cosmic order, a predetermined flow of events that may guide the broader strokes of our lives.

This duality, the coexistence of personal agency and predestined paths, is echoed in other philosophical traditions as well. The ancient Greeks, for example, grappled with similar questions through their myths and philosophies. The concept of moira or fate was central to Greek thought, yet figures like Socrates and Aristotle emphasized the role of human virtue and rationality in shaping one's destiny. They, like Krishna, believed in the power of choice, even within the bounds of a larger cosmic design.

Thus, the Bhagavad Gita, alongside other ancient philosophies, invites us to consider life as an intricate dance between free will and destiny. It suggests that while we may not have control over the cards we are dealt, we do have the power to choose how we play them. In this interplay between action and fate, between duty and destiny, life reveals itself as a complex yet beautiful tapestry, woven with threads of both choice and inevitability.

In this intricate dance of existence, life reveals itself as a tapestry woven from threads of hope and inevitability. Like two sides of a coin, our dreams and the intricate patterns of destiny intersect, shaping the very fabric of our reality. It's a delicate balance, where the strokes of our ambition paint vibrant hues upon the canvas of fate.

Amidst the triumphs and tribulations of our journey, we find ourselves embracing the euphoria of success. We celebrate the sweat and toil, the relentless pursuit of excellence that propels us forward. Each victory is a testament to our resilience, a testament to the power of human endeavor.

Yet, in the shadows of defeat, we are often tempted to relinquish agency, to seek refuge in the comforting embrace of destiny. We cast blame upon the whims of fate, surrendering to the belief that our failures were foretold. But in doing so, do we not diminish the significance of our triumphs? Can we truly claim ownership of our successes if we attribute our failures to forces beyond our control?

These are the profound quandaries that stir the depths of our consciousness, beckoning us to explore the mysteries of our existence. As we navigate the labyrinth of life, we are compelled to confront the paradoxes of agency and fate, seeking solace in the pursuit of understanding amidst the complexities of our reality.

In the intricate dance of life, success and failure share equal footing, each playing a pivotal role in shaping our journey. The chasm between envisioning a life of abundance and realizing it is vast, traversed only by those who dare to bridge the gap through action and perseverance.

Consider the student, poised on the threshold of academic pursuit, their aspirations soaring high. In the corridors of youth, failure seems a distant specter, overshadowed by the allure of success. Yet, for some, the path to achievement remains elusive, as they falter in the face of challenges unforeseen. The dream of passing exams and securing commendable grades is but a whisper in the wind, drowned out by the deafening silence of unfulfilled potential.

Why does this dissonance persist? It is because mere contemplation does not pave the way to success; action does. Those who traverse the path to success do so with unwavering determination, their steps guided by the beacon of diligence. They immerse themselves in the rigors of study, honing their skills and fortifying their resolve with each passing day. It is this relentless pursuit of excellence that propels them towards their goals, transforming lofty aspirations into tangible achievements.

Yet, for others, the dream remains but a mirage, shimmering tantalizingly on the horizon yet ever out of reach.

Similarly, in the broader landscape of life, our dreams and aspirations serve as guiding stars, illuminating the path toward our desired destinies. But it is the sweat of our brow and the resilience of our spirit that propel us forward. Those who ardently pursue their ambitions, channeling their energies into action, often find themselves reaping the fruits of their labor. Yet, for those content to merely dream without action, the chasm between vision and reality remains unbridged.

It is not merely the dreamers who triumph, but those who dare to transform their dreams into reality through the crucible of action. Life rewards those who dare to translate their aspirations into tangible endeavors.

In the intricate dance of life, destiny asserts its presence, guiding our footsteps along a preordained path, albeit for a finite duration. It is akin to a silent orchestrator, shaping the contours of our existence from the moment of our inception.

From the moment of our birth, the seeds of destiny are sown, nurtured by the hopes and aspirations of those who came before us. Our parents, with boundless love and unwavering dedication, craft a vision for our future, meticulously planning each step of our journey. In their eyes, we are the architects of our destiny, destined for greatness from the moment we draw our first breath.

In the innocence of youth, we are blissfully unaware of the intricate tapestry of fate that envelops us. Our parents, with foresight and wisdom, guide our every decision, from the mundane to the monumental. They chart a course for our lives, paving the way for a future filled with promise and possibility.

Every choice they make is imbued with love and care, fueled by a desire to provide us with the best possible start in life. From the food we eat to the clothes we wear, from the schools we attend to the friends we keep, their influence knows no bounds. And in their hands, we find solace and security, knowing that they will always steer us toward the path of righteousness and fulfillment.

Yet, as we journey through the labyrinth of life, we inevitably come face to face with the reality of our own agency. Gradually, we begin to discern the subtle nuances of the world around us, forging our own path in defiance of fate's gentle guidance. With each passing day, we assert our independence, making choices that may diverge from the path laid out by our parents.

It is in these moments of divergence that the true nature of destiny reveals itself. For destiny is not a fixed point in time but rather a fluid and ever-changing force, shaped by the interplay of our choices and circumstances. As we navigate the complexities of adulthood, we realize that our destiny is not preordained but rather forged through the crucible of our own actions.

And so, we embrace the duality of fate and free will, recognizing that while destiny may set the stage, it is ultimately our choices that determine the outcome.

The odyssey of destiny commences at this juncture, where the threads of fate intertwine with the tapestry of our lives. Should the courses charted for us lead to triumph, we bask in the glow of our own ingenuity and diligence. But should misfortune befall us, the blame is swiftly cast upon the shoulders of destiny.

In much the same way, when we first tread upon this earthly realm, it is not without purpose or design. God, in His infinite wisdom, has woven a tapestry of existence, each thread meticulously crafted with care and foresight. To Him, we are all cherished children, and He looks upon us with boundless love and compassion

As long as we heed the divine guidance set forth by God and adhere to His grand design, our journey unfolds with grace and serenity. His teachings serve as a beacon of light, illuminating the path to righteousness and fulfillment. He implores us to conduct ourselves with integrity and sincerity, to never stray from the path of righteousness for personal gain.

Destiny, akin to a meticulously scripted notebook, serves as the repository of our future, each page adorned with the divine blueprint of our existence. Much like how we inscribe our aspirations and intentions in a personal diary, detailing the tasks we aim to accomplish in the days, months, and years ahead, and destiny delineates the course of our lives with unfathomable precision.

Yet, much like the plans we outline in our diaries, the fruition of destiny's design hinges upon our actions and choices. The realization of these predetermined events is contingent upon our proactive engagement and decisive actions. Just as our plans materialize only when we actively pursue them, destiny's manifestations unfold when we align our actions with its script. Should we deviate from the prescribed path or fail to realize the intentions inscribed within destiny's pages, alterations and amendments inevitably ensue, reshaping the contours of our future with each decision we make.

The notion that individuals script their own destinies echoes through the corridors of wisdom. While I am inclined to believe in the predetermined course of destiny, I am equally convinced that human agency possesses the transformative power to shape the course of destiny. As I've elucidated earlier, life unfolds at the nexus of fate and action, with karma and destiny intertwining to weave the fabric of our existence.

Indeed, life's tapestry is imbued with the intricate threads of karma and destiny, each contributing its unique hue to the tableau of human experience. Half of our journey is steered by the rudder of karma, our actions rippling through the currents of fate, while destiny casts its indelible shadow upon the other half.

For those who find solace in the harmonious cadence of their lives, where each melody resonates with the chords of righteousness and integrity, it is a testament to their alignment with the divine plan. In such instances, one's deeds become a symphony of consequences, orchestrated in consonance with the benevolent script penned by the divine hand. However, for those who find themselves at odds with the unfolding narrative of their lives, where reality diverges from the dreams they once fervently held, casting blame upon fate can seem like a natural reflex. Yet, navigating a course towards reshaping the tapestry of their destiny necessitates a profound introspection and a willingness to recalibrate their ambitions.

The yearning for redemption often stirs within us a profound desire for a second chance—a chance to rewrite the script of our lives with the wisdom garnered from past missteps. There's a palpable longing in the human spirit, a fervent wish to navigate life's labyrinthine pathways with greater clarity and purpose. We find ourselves contemplating the hypotheticals: if given another life, another opportunity, how would we sculpt our existence differently?

But what if I told you that you hold the power to rewrite your story? That the narrative of your life is not set in stone, but rather a fluid tapestry woven from the fabric of your choices and actions?

Consider this: every morning heralds a new beginning, a chance to turn the tide and chart a different course. As the first rays of sunlight pierce through the darkness, illuminating the world with their golden glow, we are presented with an opportunity to shape our destiny anew. With each breath, with each heartbeat, we are presented with an opportunity—a chance to breathe life into our aspirations, to mold our reality with the deft strokes of intention and purpose. It's a reminder that we are not merely passive spectators in the theater of fate but active participants, co-creators of our own narratives.

It's a sentiment echoed by those who yearn for a second chance, a shot at redemption in the face of past mistakes. With each sunrise comes the promise of transformation, the possibility to break free from the shackles of fate and carve out a path of our own making.

As the evening sky darkens and the stars begin to twinkle, no one lies down to sleep with the thought that they might not wake up the next morning. Instead, each person, regardless of their circumstances, tucks themselves into bed with a heart full of hope and a mind brimming with plans for the coming day. In the quiet moments before sleep takes over, people dream of their future. They envision the tasks they'll accomplish, the conversations they'll have, and the goals they'll pursue. Their minds dance with the possibilities of what tomorrow could bring. The anticipation of a new day fuels their spirit, allowing them to drift into a restful slumber.

But life, in its unpredictable nature, often has other plans. For some, the dreams woven in the night are left unrealized as they do not awaken with the dawn. The plans remain unfulfilled, and the dreams linger in the space between night and day, a poignant reminder of life's fleeting nature. So, if fate has dealt you a hand that doesn't align with your aspirations, don't lose heart. Instead, seize the dawn with renewed determination, knowing that the power to reshape your destiny lies within your grasp. Embrace the gift of each new day, and let your actions pave the way to a future filled with hope, purpose, and fulfillment.

In our minds, there often lingers the thought that we haven't achieved what we desired in life, leading us to believe that perhaps it's too late. We find ourselves pondering whether the sands of time have slipped through our fingers, leaving behind only the echo of missed opportunities.

Every endeavor has its opportune moment, and it seems right only at that time. However, if things haven't unfolded as we wished, it doesn't necessarily mean that the significance of those aspirations in our lives has ceased to exist, or that we can no longer attain them. It's possible that the time hasn't come yet, perhaps the stars have yet to align, or perhaps we haven't put in the required effort to attain those desires.

Consider, for instance, the simple act of planting a tree and reaping its fruits. When is the optimal time to have set the seed into the soil? Perhaps five- or ten-years past. But even now, as we stand amidst the barren earth, it's not too late. Today, as we plant the sapling, we sow the seeds of tomorrow's bounty. Yet, nurturing such growth demands patience, dedication, and a meticulous hand.

Just as a gardener tends to their orchard, diligently watering and nourishing each shoot, so too must we care for the garden of our lives. Weeding out the weeds of negativity, pruning away the branches of self-doubt, we create space for the blossoms of possibility to bloom. With each tender touch and every nurturing gesture, we cultivate a landscape rich with promise, a sanctuary where dreams take root and flourish. In much the same way, the choices we make today are like seeds planted in the fertile soil of our future; each decision, every action, serves as a step in shaping the destiny we seek to cultivate.